★ ★ ★ CHICAGO ★ ★ ★

BASEBALL *in the* CITY

Joe Crede of the White Sox takes a cut in an interleague game with the Cubs on June 26, 2005. The Cubs won the game, 2–0.

★ ★ ★ ★ CHICAGO ★ ★ ★ ★
BASEBALL *in the* CITY

By Derek Gentile ★ Foreword by Studs Terkel

THUNDER BAY
P·R·E·S·S
San Diego, California

Thunder Bay Press

An imprint of the Advantage Publishers Group
5880 Oberlin Drive, San Diego, CA 92121-4794
www.thunderbaybooks.com

All notations of errors or omissions should be addressed to Thunder Bay Press, Editorial Department, at the above address. All other correspondence (author inquiries, permissions) concerning the content of this book should be addressed to becker&mayer!, 11010 Northup Way, Bellevue, Washington, 98004, infobm@beckermayer.com

Chicago: Baseball in the City is produced by becker&mayer!, Bellevue, Washington. www.beckermayer.com

Design: Paul Barrett
Editorial: Avra Romanowitz and Conor Risch
Image Research: Shayna Ian and Chris Campbell
Production Coordination: Adrian Lucia

ISBN-13:   978-1-59223-576-6
ISBN-10:   1-59223-576-X

Library of Congress Cataloging-in-Publication Data

Gentile, Derek.
    Chicago baseball in the city / by Derek Gentile.
        p. cm.
    ISBN-13: 978-1-59223-576-6
    ISBN-10: 1-59223-576-X
    1. Baseball—Illinois—Chicago. I. Title.

GV863.G46 2006
796.35709773'11-dc22
                                                        2005055925

Printed in China

1 2 3 4 5 10 09 08 07 06

This book is dedicated to Chicago baseball fans everywhere,
and also to Joseph Jefferson Jackson of Brandon Mills, South Carolina.
May he rest in peace.

On April 19, 1949, the Chicago Cubs hosted the Pirates at Wrigley Field for their season opener.

Table of Contents

8.   **Foreword by Studs Terkel**

10.   **Introduction**

The Leagues and the Teams

14.   *The Chicago Cubs*

44.   *The Chicago White Sox*

76.   *Little League*

81.   *The Chicago Whales*

84.   *The Negro Leagues*

94.   *The All-American Girls Professional Baseball League*

The Places

102.   *Home of the Cubs*

107.   *Home of the White Sox*

112.   *The Top Ten Most Dramatic Moments in Chicago Baseball History*

116.   *The Top Ten Most Disappointing Moments in Chicago Baseball History*

The People

122.   *All-Time All-Stars*

142.   *Hometown Heroes: The Minors*

146.   *Hometown Heroes: Chicago-born Major Leaguers*

156.   *The Broadcasters*

160.   *The Fans*

168.   **Conclusion**

170.   **Index**

Foreword ★ ★ ★

BY STUDS TERKEL

Studs Terkel is a Pulitzer Prize–winning author, longtime radio broadcaster, and one of America's literary lions. He is also as closely tied to Chicago as the El and Lake Michigan. In addition to his lifelong love of the American people and of telling—or helping them to tell—their stories, he has a love of baseball. He was a commentator in the famous 1994 Ken Burns documentary Baseball, *and he portrayed Chicago sportswriter Hugh Fullerton in the 1988 film* Eight Men Out, *about the 1919 Chicago "Black Sox" scandal. Mr. Terkel reflects here on his memories of baseball in general and the game in Chicago in particular.*

My earliest baseball memory is from 1920. I was still living in New York then—I didn't come to Chicago until shortly thereafter. I was eight years old, and the Indians beat the Dodgers in the World Series. The Indians second baseman, Bill Wambsganss, performed the only unassisted triple play in World Series history. That name proved useful to me, as I worked to deal with childhood asthma and a real fear of falling asleep. To ease my passage into sleep, I took to speaking names of well-known people as a way to calm me down, and baseball proved to be a big part of this plan. As I wrote in my book *Will the Circle Be Unbroken?*, the names of players from that 1920 Series were part of this nighttime routine:

Stanley Coveleski, the Indians' pitcher, who had won three games. Stan-ley Cov-el-es-ki. Six salubrious syllables. The peerless Tris Speaker, who covered center field like a comfortable quilt. Bill Wambsganss, the second baseman, who pulled off the unassisted triple play. Wambsganss. The name's slow pronunciation had the pleasant, slumberous effect of a Dutch hot chocolate. Some thirty years later, when a television program with which I was involved, *Studs' Place*, went off the air, I received a scrawled, handwritten letter from Cleveland. I remember a passage: "I enjoyed your program because it gave me a feeling of *heimweh*, an old Dutch word for homesickness. I was once a baseball player. They called me Wamby." It was signed Bill Wambsganss. I replied, though I neglected to tell him how he had helped me through my insomnia.

Those are my earliest memories of baseball. As for Chicago baseball, I don't remember the Black Sox scandal myself; I was only seven. But I came to Chicago not long after and began to hear much about it.

★ 8 ★

Eight players were kicked out, as we all know, but it should have been nine—owner Charles Comiskey should have been kicked out as well. His actions made the players easy marks for the gamblers. For instance, he had promised star pitcher Eddie Cicotte a $10,000 bonus for winning thirty games. But when Cicotte won twenty-eight games, Comiskey ordered the manager, Kid Gleason, to bench Cicotte so he could not earn the bonus.

I was a Giants fan as a kid, so I couldn't be a Cubs fan,[1] though I do remember my first game at Wrigley Field. They had just done a trade with the Phillies and had acquired Bill Killefer as catcher-manager along with Grover Cleveland Alexander.

I liked the White Sox because they were so pathetic and ragamuffin. They were awfully bad around that time (1920s–1930s). They had Early Sheely at first, for instance. He was so bad we thought he had a wooden leg. There were also lots of players with such great names, like Smead Jolley. How could you *not* root for a team with Smead Jolley on it? There was also Bibb Falk, the fine outfielder.

Another thing I remember is watching the electric scoreboards outside the department stores. This was before TV, of course, so crowds would gather to stand and watch this board updated via telegraph and telephone. I stood out there for Game 3—or was it 4?—of the 1929 World Series, Cubs vs. the Philadelphia Athletics. I remember that the Cubs were up 8–0 and then Hack Wilson lost a fly ball in the sun. They ended up losing 10–8.

---

1. Ed. note: the clubs were then archrivals in the eight-team National League.

Chicago has had two baseball teams since the turn of the twentieth century. Cubs games remain more as events than ballgames. It's more about going to a place than watching a baseball game. You ask afterward who won and they don't know.

As for the White Sox World Series championship, well, it was so unexpected. I'm delighted. I think all Chicago baseball fans are thrilled, really. I think the idea that the city has been altered was exaggerated. People like a winner, that's true. But the Cubs will still draw; it doesn't matter whether they win or lose, they'll fill the park. As long as the Sox win, they will, too. But they won't repeat as champions unless they get a third bat in the lineup! ★

Introduction ★ ★ ★

Baseball started out about 150 years ago as a pastoral game, played on open fields of grass by gentlemen. But it soon found its truest and best life played by workingmen in the gritty cities. As the game moved from amateur pastime to national obsession in the 1870s, one of the first places where baseball found a loving home was the City of the Big Shoulders . . . which, as it happens, are a pretty good tool to have to play the game. Chicago may have the somewhat undeserved reputation as "America's Second City," but it stands second to none when it comes to baseball history and tradition.

There's a reason the Chicago Cubs have remained in the same city since 1876. There's a reason Ban Johnson, the founder of the American League, insisted in 1900 that his league have a franchise in Chicago to go head-to-head with the Cubs. There's a reason the Negro Leagues played their all-star games at Comiskey Park. And there's a reason the All-American Girls Professional Baseball League was based in Chicago.

People in Chicago love the game.

Yes, they love the Bulls, and there is a core group of fans that love the Bears. But as Albert Spalding, an early Chicago star pitcher, pointed out, "Once the germ of baseball gets in one's blood, it is impossible to get it out." And, there is no doubt that Chicago has had the fever for more than a century.

Fans around the world know baseball in Chi-town. Chicago baseball is South Side vs. North Side, it's Ernie Banks "playin' two," it's Harry Caray bellowing from the Wrigley bleachers. Chicago baseball is neighborhoods and family and tradition. Chicago baseball is exploding scoreboards, disco demolition, and curse-laying goats.

But while many people are aware of the grand history and unique traditions of pro baseball in the Windy City, most are not as knowledgeable about the game away from the bright lights (well, after 1988, that is . . . see page 105) of the pro game. Chicago baseball is also the Rockford Peaches and Chicago Colleens, it's a bunch of kids from Roseland trying to defeat the young stars from Tokyo, and it's a little-known pro league that died a quick death but left an ivy-covered legacy.

This book is about all of that and more. Take it out to the ball game, take it out with the crowd, if you want; we've got home teams aplenty to root for in here. Grab a red hot, pop a beer, and enjoy. ★

The Leagues
and the Teams

The Chicago Cubs ★ ★ ★

What can we say about the Chicago Cubs that has not been said, sung, lamented, and/or cried about for most of the nearly one hundred years since they last won a World Series? Chicago might be home to two Major League teams—the other being the White Sox, of course—but it is home to only one *legendary* Major League team: the Cubbies. (Pipe down, South Siders . . . you'll get your due shortly.) The Cubs are the ultimate lovable losers. The quintessential "almost-but-not-quites." A team that annually earns enough love to fill Wrigleyville from April to September but then nearly as annually leaves October a dull, gray void. We won't even mention the off-season.

The Cubs have been part of big-league baseball, in various forms, since Ulysses S. Grant was president. And like Grant, they started out winners, with a couple of titles in the early twentieth century, the first full century of what is today Major League Baseball. But after 1908—nothing. No championships, not even a trip to the World Series since 1945. A record of unachievement unmatched in the annals of the grand old game. Yet amid this record of, well . . . failure, somehow the Cubs have also become perhaps the most beloved team in the sport. To what do we owe this contradiction, wonder the pundits. Some would point

to America's love of the underdog, of the belief that every Cub will somehow have its day . . . eventually. Others point to Wrigley Field (page 102), the team's longtime home, a reminder of happier, simpler days and the site of baseball's most intimate urban experience (take that, Yankee Stadium!). You could also look to the team's many stars over the years, players whose accomplishments should have earned them championship rings but who were left instead with nothing but cheers: Banks, Santo, Jenkins, Sandberg, Sutcliffe, Sosa, et al. Whatever the reason or the cause, the truth remains: win or lose, Chicago (and the baseball world in general, truth be told) loves its Cubbies. "We could win seven World Series in a row," said White Sox manager Ozzie Guillen in 2005, as his team worked on the first of that proposed streak, "and this town would still belong to the Cubs."

So, on to the historical record. The story records losses and a few wins, and it tells of heroes of old and legends of today. It points to the story of what happened on the field for more than 120 years. But underneath all the stats, beyond all the scores, remember the feeling of walking beneath the El down West Addison Street, hearing the soft roar of a gathering crowd on a sunny afternoon, and seeing the bright red sign

that shows you've arrived at a place called Wrigley Field and are about to become part of an ongoing baseball story.

Sure, the Cubs haven't won in forever. So what? Let's play two!

Starting with the Stockings

The original Chicago Cubs franchise was founded in 1870 as the Chicago White Stockings, a semipro club formed to compete with the better-known Cincinnati Red Stockings. In 1871, the White Stockings, along with seven other teams, formed the National Association, which is generally recognized as the first real major league.

Manager Jimmy Wood, a Brooklynite who played second base and had a batting average of .378, led the team in its first season. On October 8, 1871, while the White Stockings were in a tight race for the pennant, the Great Chicago Fire broke out. The team's stadium right off Michigan Avenue was destroyed, as were all of their uniforms and equipment. Incredibly, the White Stockings finished the season only two games behind that year's champions, the Philadelphia Athletics.

The homeless White Stockings disbanded for two years before their return in 1874. But they were not the team they had been, finishing 28–31 and eighteen games out of first that year. The squad did even worse in 1875, ending up 30–37 and thirty-five games out.

By 1875, the baseball world was on the eve of change. White Stockings president William A. Hulbert and Boston Red Stockings pitcher Albert Spalding were conspiring to start a new and more organized league.

Al Spalding was a great pitcher, leading the National Association in wins from 1872 to 1875 and his Boston franchise to pennant victories all four of those years. Spalding was an even better businessman, though. He realized that the National Association, a loose conglomeration of teams with wildly varying financial means, would collapse sooner or later. It was not uncommon in those early years for teams to fold midseason or for players to jump squads with impunity. Spalding wanted to change that. He wanted to play baseball with a more stable group of franchises.

Soon after the close of the 1875 season, Spalding secretly signed a contract with the White Stockings and convinced three other Boston stars to join him—catcher Jim "Deacon" White, first baseman Cal McVey, and second baseman Ross Barnes.

With the addition of these four former Boston players and with Spalding's financial backing, Hulbert began negotiating with a cadre of businessmen from several cities to launch franchises as part of a new "national league" that would be better run and better financed than the National Association.

It all happened in a remarkably short amount of time. Baseball was becoming extremely popular, and there were a lot of businessmen who wanted to own a big-league franchise and cash in on this new national obsession.

The National League

By the beginning of 1876, the National League was officially born, and it intended to settle into cities large enough (populations of 75,000 or more) for sizable fan bases. The new league was comprised of franchises based in eight major American cities: Chicago, St. Louis, Boston, Louisville, New York, Philadelphia, Cincinnati, and Hartford.

Stocked with great ballplayers, including Spalding and his three former Boston teammates, Chicago walked away with the first National League pennant. Spalding, as player-manager, went 47–12 on the mound. Second baseman and star hitter Ross Barnes ripped up opposing pitchers and won the batting crown with a .429 average, sixty-three points higher than the second-place finisher. Barnes's mark that year remains a team record well over a century later.

White's sixty RBIs led the league, and star newcomer Adrian Anson

led the league's third basemen in putouts (135), assists (147), and double plays (9).

Meanwhile, Al Spalding, along with his younger brother, J. Walter Spalding, began a sporting-goods business in town. The store carried equipment and clothing and became the Spalding sporting-goods empire.

The next season was a little less successful for the team as Spalding, his arm worn down after six years of hard use, moved from the pitcher's mound to first base. To save his hands, he began wearing a black leather glove with the fingers cut out and a padded palm on his left, or catching, hand. Up to this point, ballplayers had played bare-handed, as using a glove was considered amateurish. But when the great Al Spalding started wearing a mitt, others began experimenting with them, too. Spalding's Sporting Store was only too happy to supply players with the new mitts and, for a while, was the only company that made them. Spalding's also began manufacturing baseballs, and Al and Walter made a fortune those first few years.

The Chicago team was hot, but others soon caught up. Boston Red Stockings manager Harry Wright had replenished his team, and they won the pennant in 1877 and 1878, and finished second in 1879 as the White Stockings floundered.

Adrian Anson took over the managerial reins from Spalding, who became the team's general manager while he devoted more of his time to the sporting-goods business. At six feet, 210 pounds, Anson was

initially nicknamed "Baby" for his fresh-faced looks. He was an exceptional athlete. The big guy would play first base most of his career but could play virtually any position, including pitcher. He quickly began building the team back up, acquiring third baseman Edward "Ned" Williamson and outfielders George Gore, Abner Dalrymple, and Michael "King" Kelly.

Kelly was the key; one of the best athletes of the nineteenth century, he spent two years with Cincinnati before signing with Chicago. An excellent hitter and a strong leader, Kelly was one of the smartest players in the game. He was never above a little gamesmanship, either. In those days, the league used only one umpire, who would position himself behind the pitcher to call balls and strikes. If Kelly was the runner on first base, he would often cut from first to third on a deep fly ball while the umpire scuttled into the outfield to determine what was happening and make a call.

A Contest Begins

At the end of the 1885 season, the White Stockings reluctantly agreed to a series of games against the American Association champion St. Louis Brown Stockings. That is, Anson and Spalding agreed to the games. The players, led by Gore and Kelly, believed their contracts ended at the conclusion of the regular season. They had no intention of playing any more games that year but were finally browbeaten by Anson into participating.

What would eventually evolve into the biggest contest in baseball started under woefully inauspicious circumstances. The Chicago papers called the games "exhibitions," while the St. Louis papers declared the games were for the "National Championship of Base Ball." Regardless, the series saw three wins for each team, and one tie. Pitcher John Clarkson tried to get out of pitching in one of the games by showing up so drunk that he passed out in the dugout. Kelly and several other players showed up for another game two hours early because they had been up all night drinking and decided to just sleep it off in the clubhouse. Most of the players didn't take the postseason games too seriously at best—and at worst, they were outright incensed by what they saw as a breach of their contracts.

The games themselves were not very well attended, in either Chicago or St. Louis. At the time, teams often played postseason exhibitions and such contests were perceived by a vast majority of fans as games of no particular significance. None of the games drew more than 3,000 fans, and one game attracted only 500 spectators.

Chicago won the pennant again the next year, finishing 90–34, two and a half games ahead of Detroit. Clarkson pitched a mortal 36–17, while McCormick went 31–11. Once again, at the end of the season there was an exhibition series with the American Association champion Brown Stockings. And, once again, Kelly did not want to participate. He did, of course, but he and several other Chicago players were keeping late hours, and this time St. Louis won the series, four games to two.

Spalding didn't really care much about the exhibition series. What he did care about was that Kelly was becoming disruptive. Before the 1887 season, Kelly was sold to Boston for $10,000. It was the largest cash transaction in league history up to that time. Spalding also sold Gore, another carouser, this time to the Giants.

Chicago suffered on the field as a result of those sales, coming close to the pennant several times in the next few years but never winning it. In Boston, the story was different. With Kelly leading the way, they won the flag in 1891, 1892, and 1893.

A Century Ends

Even without Kelly's help, the White Stockings were competitive most years until 1900, but they never won another pennant during that span. Anson was, if not the best player in the National League, the most prominent. Yet by the 1890s he was getting a little long in the tooth, and Spalding was devoting almost all of his time to his store. So, in

1891, Spalding asked a business acquaintance, James A. Hart, to run the day-to-day operations of the team.

Spalding went out of his way, both publicly and privately, to assure Anson that he was still the individual who would make the on-field decisions. But Big Cap didn't like sharing his role. He and Hart were soon openly feuding.

Although Chicago had signed several solid players (including outfielder Bill Lange, shortstop Bill Dahlen, and pitcher Clark Griffith), by the end of 1897 the team—now called the Colts by sportswriters for its youthful roster—was floundering. Spalding decided it was time to make a move. While Anson was on a tour of Europe, Spalding named veteran Tommy Burns manager. Spalding never took the time to alert Anson he'd been canned, leaving the ex-manager to discover his new status upon his return.

It was clearly a tough call for Spalding. Anson had managed the team for nineteen years and set the franchise record for career hits (2,995). He had been Spalding's closest ally during the team's early years, yet Cap was forty-five that year, an age at which many nineteenth-century athletes were either long retired or dead. Everyone but Anson knew he had to go. Still, a little personal attention from Spalding was called for, and it didn't happen.

A New Century: The 1900s

All the hurt feelings involved in Anson's sacking didn't even amount to a successful change—Burns wasn't a good manager. The team's next notable season didn't come until 1906, by which time Spalding was devoting himself completely to sporting goods, and the young team was dubbed the Cubs by local newspapermen. The name is one of the longest-running aliases in sports history.

The 1906 team led the league in ERA with a 1.75 mark, almost a half-run better than the next team, the New York Giants. They scored a league-best 705 runs and allowed just 381. With savvy players like tough shortstop Joe Tinker, muscular first baseman Frank "Husk" Chance, and second baseman Johnny Evers, the Cubs seemed invincible going into the World Series.

They were not.

The crosstown White Sox had won the American League pennant.

The Sox had great pitching and defense but only mediocre hitting, which gave them the nickname "the Hitless Wonders." Though heavily favored in the Series, the Cubs lost, four games to two. The White Sox had two hot pitchers, Nick Altrock and "Big" Ed Walsh, who won three of the four games. Second baseman Frank Isbell gave an amazing performance: a career .250 hitter, he batted .308 in the Series. Isbell contributed in game one with an RBI single and exploded for four doubles in game five to help the Sox win 8–6. With the help of strong pitching, the Hitless Wonders performed a miracle, winning the Series. The Cubs had to watch their rivals celebrate on streets that belonged to both teams. It was a hard pill to swallow.

The Cubs bounced back in 1907 to easily capture the pennant again. This time, they faced the Detroit Tigers and superstar Ty Cobb in the Series. Cobb boasted that he would steal the Cubs blind on the base paths, but it didn't happen. Johnny Kling threw out seven Tigers trying to steal, Cobb had no stolen bases, and the Cubs beat the Tigers in five games, including one tie.

The 1908 Cubs were also favored to take the pennant, which they did, but it wasn't as easy as in the previous two years. The New York Giants, with pitcher Christy Mathewson, and the Pittsburgh Pirates, with shortstop Honus Wagner, made it a race. The three teams exchanged first place throughout the season. The Giants seemed to be in command by September, but on the twenty-third of that month, the season's most controversial game took place.

Who's on Second?

The Cubs were at New York on an unseasonably warm Wednesday afternoon. With the score 1–1 in the ninth inning, Giant outfielder Harry "Moose" McCormick was on first. Rookie Fred Merkle was at the plate, and he singled to put men at first and third with two outs.

Next up was pinch hitter Al Bridwell. With the crowd roaring, Bridwell drilled a single up the middle. McCormick clapped his hands

and trotted home with the winning run. Merkle started toward second base but saw a crowd of joyous Giant fans hopping the fences, so he veered off the base paths and headed to the New York clubhouse.

The Cubs' Johnny Evers, at second, saw what had happened. With a man on first and two outs, the player must touch second base,

according to the rules. If the inning ends on a force play, the runs cannot be counted. Evers shouted to outfielder Solly Hofman to get the ball, which had rolled into the outfield. There was a scuffle with a fan, but the ball went to Evers. Meanwhile, first baseman Frank Chance grabbed umpire Hank O'Day to make sure he saw Evers touch second base. He had, but news accounts of the day (depending on the allegiance

of the source) vary as to whether or not he actually made the "out" call. At any rate, O'Day declared the game a tie a few hours later. If necessary, there would be a replay at the end of the season.

It was a controversy that engulfed the country. Most papers, even those in New York, ripped Merkle for not touching second base. The so-called Merkle's Boner was a play he would live with until the day he died.

McGraw never blamed Merkle. He blamed the umpire for being gutless. The game, he insisted, was truly over. Johnny Evers touching second base nearly twenty minutes after the fact was a circus trick. For Cubs fans, the rules were the rules. In fact, Chance, in a rather gutsy move, insisted that the game be forfeited to Chicago because the Giants left the field early. No such luck. Of course, the season ended in a tie and the Cubs were required to return to New York to replay the game.

Talk about a circus. The Giants' Polo Grounds were packed to the rafters, and several thousand fans surged against the gates, trying to get in. Several Cubs players even received death threats.

No matter. The Cubs' Mordecai "Three Finger" Brown pitched eight superb innings after relieving Jack Pfiester during the first inning. Chance, who had been ducking bottles, coins, and stones all day from

his post at first base, drilled an RBI double in the third to make the score 4–1, Cubs.

That was it. The Giants scratched a run off Brown late in the game, but as the sun began to set that afternoon in New York, the Chicago Cubs had won their third consecutive pennant.

"Tinker to Evers to Chance"

Chicago now faced the American League champion Detroit Tigers in the Series. Chicago won four of the five contests to claim its second— and, to this day, last—World Series title. The Cubs also became the first team to win back-to-back World Series championships. Life was good, and the nervous wondered when it would end. Their time would have been better spent savoring their present good fortune.

Certainly, there were a few good years left in this core group. The Cubs won the pennant in 1910, losing the World Series to the Philadelphia Athletics. That was also the year that New York writer Franklin Pierce Adams, a big Giants fan, was getting a little sick of his lads losing to the Chicago nine. And there seemed, to Adams, to be three Cubbies in particular who were responsible. So he penned what he called a "bit of doggerel" about the Cub infield and what is commonly known as "Baseball's Sad Lexicon."

These are the saddest of possible words,
Tinker to Evers to Chance.
Trio of bear cubs, and fleeter than birds,
Tinker to Evers to Chance.
Thoughtlessly pricking our gonfalon bubble,
Making a Giant hit into a double,
Words that are weighty with nothing but trouble—
Tinker to Evers to Chance.

It was not the greatest poem in the world. ("Gonfalon," by the way, is an old word for "flag" or "pennant.") But it was short, it was catchy, and people could recite it pretty easily. It is the most famous poem about real ballplayers ever written. ("Casey at the Bat" was fictional.)

Ironically, 1910 was the last year the trio played together full-time. In 1911, the pitching staff began to age, Evers was injured, and Chance became a part-time player. The Cubs slowly began to slide in the standings.

Three's a Crowd: The 1910s

Murphy sold the team to another local businessman, Charles Taft, before the 1914 season. But across town, another businessman, Charles Weeghman, was doing a bang-up job with his Chicago Whales team, part of the newly formed Federal League (see page 81).

The short-lived Federal League was dissolved after 1915, but Weeghman was not finished with baseball. He bought out Taft and combined players from the Whales and the Cubs to create the beginnings of a team that would go on to win the 1918 National League pennant. The revamped Cubs moved over to play at Weeghman Park, which would later become known as Wrigley Field.

Albert Spalding died in September of 1915. A premier pitcher in the 1870s and an organizational master of baseball, Spalding led the Cubs to seven pennants before leaving the team to grow his business.

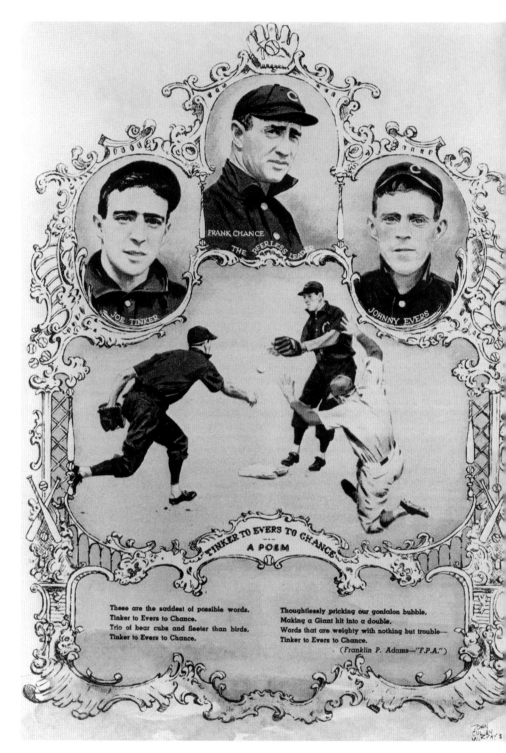

The 1918 Cubs had a formidable pitching staff: James "Hippo" Vaughn, Claude Hendrix, and George "Lefty" Tyler. In addition, manning first base was none other than Fred Merkle, who had been picked up from the Brooklyn Robins the previous year. Sometimes, there's no better cure for a haunting mistake than going straight into the belly of the beast.

The Cubs' opponents in the Series had a few pitchers of their own. The Boston Red Sox boasted five starters, including Carl Mays, "Bullet" Joe Bush, Dutch Leonard, "Sad" Sam Jones, and a big lefty named George Herman "Babe" Ruth.

Ruth and Mays won two games each in the Series, leading the Red Sox to victory, four games to two. Boston would not win another title until 2004.

By 1918, Weeghman wanted out. Professional baseball was an expensive proposition, and he wasn't financially solvent enough to keep going. With this in mind, he began negotiations with one of his minority partners, William Wrigley.

Wrigley's Team: The 1920s

Wrigley, the son of a soap maker, was a successful, self-made businessman. He had begun a sales career as a teen and had built his father's business into a thriving concern. When he was approached by Weeghman in 1915 to be a minority partner, he jumped at the chance. By 1919, he had made enough money to buy Weeghman out. In 1926, the park was renamed Wrigley Field in honor of its owner. Today it is the second oldest ballpark in the majors behind Boston's Fenway Park.

Wrigley loved the game but publicly admitted that he didn't know much about running a baseball team. In those early years of Wrigley ownership, the Cubs didn't have many strong players. So, in 1920, Wrigley hired former sportswriter Bill Veeck Sr. to run the show.

Veeck was an innovative marketer who, in 1927, sold the radio broadcast rights to Cubs' games in an era when most owners thought that such a move ensured bankruptcy. Owners feared if the games were broadcast, fans would stay away from the ballpark and just listen to the radio instead. Yet one day in 1927, while in the Cubs' parking lot, Veeck noticed hundreds of out-of-state license plates. Rather than keeping people home, Veeck realized, the broadcasts reached a wider fan base and sparked interest from home and afar.

Veeck came up with Ladies Day in 1929. During designated games (usually midweek tilts that were generally lightly attended), women were allowed into the ballpark for free. Attendance soared. In fact, so many women came to the games that Veeck and Wrigley had to limit the number of free seats available to the women.

By 1929, the team was ready. Manager Joe McCarthy and Veeck had a good stable but realized they needed a player to put them over the top. That player was Rogers Hornsby, one of the best right-handed hitters in the history of baseball. Hornsby's .424 batting average in 1924 remains the highest average in modern National League history.

The "Rajah," as he was called by sportswriters, had a prickly side. He was blunt and outspoken, a nasty combination. Still, his acquisition by the Cubs in 1929 was clearly the key for the team. Hornsby was the MVP of the league in 1929, hitting .380 with thirty-nine homers and 149 RBI.

The Cubs easily won the 1929 National League pennant, but their opponent in the World Series was the Philadelphia Athletics. The Athletics boasted the best pitcher in baseball in Lefty Grove and future Hall of Famers Jimmie Foxx at first base, Al Simmons in the outfield, and Mickey "Black Mike" Cochrane behind the plate. Another starter, George Earnshaw, also happened to be having a career year.

The Athletics won the first two games. Pitcher Guy Bush picked up a 3–1 win in game three, and then came the fourth game. The Cubs had been throttling the A's 8–0 through seven innings when Simmons belted a home run off Charlie Root, and the carnage began.

Five of the next six Athletics stroked singles off Root, and the Philly fans, who had been booing their team a few innings before, came to life. McCarthy pulled Root and inserted veteran Art Nehf, who hadn't pitched in weeks.

Nehf got George "Mule" Haas to pop up to outfielder Lewis Robert "Hack" Wilson, but Hack lost the ball in the sun. It rolled all the way to the wall for an inside-the-park, three-run homer. The Cubs lead was now, incredibly, 8–7. The Athletics scored three more times before finally making an out.

The Cubs players were stunned. Wilson sat in the corner of the dugout, motionless. Chicago went down meekly in the eighth and ninth innings.

The Cubs blew game five in equally heartbreaking fashion, taking a 2–0 lead into the bottom of the ninth before losing, 3–2, on a walk-off double by Philadelphia's Bing Miller. Wilson was seen sobbing on the train home to Chicago that night.

The loss had even more repercussions. Wrigley, who had previously embraced McCarthy, irrationally blamed him for the Cubs' collapse. He began criticizing McCarthy as the Cubs struggled the next year. Late in the 1930 season, McCarthy bowed to the inevitable and resigned. Wrigley immediately promoted Hornsby as manager.

Turning Over: The 1930s

The prickly Rajah was rough on rookies, and most of his veteran teammates didn't think much of him either. They thought even less of him when he began hitting them up for loans so he could play the horses, a well-known weakness of his.

The team slumped in 1930, but Wilson rebounded from his embarrassing gaffe in the 1929 World Series with a vengeance. He crushed fifty-six home runs, a National League record until Mark McGwire's seventy dingers in 1998, and had 191 RBI, a Major League record that still stands. Despite Wilson's outstanding performance, the Cubs finished second, two games out.

The 1931 season was even worse, with the Cubs finishing third, seventeen games out. At age sixty-nine, William Wrigley died, and his son, Phillip K. Wrigley (known as P.K.), took over. It would prove a turning point for the franchise.

P.K. was learning the ropes while Veeck continued to hunt for talent. The Cubs picked up shortstop Billy Jurges, second baseman Billy Herman, and third sacker Stanley Hack. Pitcher Lon Warneke, dubbed "the Arkansas Hummingbird," anchored the pitching staff along with Pat Malone, Guy Bush, and Charlie Root.

In 1932, the Cubs were quick out of the gate but sputtering by midseason. Hornsby was still hitting up the players for money, and finally, two-thirds of the way through the season, Wrigley had to fire him. Everyone, except the half-dozen players to whom he owed an estimated $10,000 in total, was happy.

The new manager was first baseman Charlie Grimm. Unlike Hornsby, "Jolly Cholly," as he was called, never admonished a player in public. And, unlike Hornsby, if the team played poorly, Grimm would shrug and remind everyone that there was another game to play the next day.

It worked. The Cubs rallied past the Pirates and Dodgers to win the pennant by four games.

The World Series was another story.

The 1932 New York Yankees, the American League champs, had nine future Hall of Famers on their roster. This impressive lineup included outfielders Earle Combs and Babe Ruth (converted from a pitcher to an outfielder before being sold from the Red Sox to the Yankees); pitchers Red Ruffing, Lefty Gomez, and Herb Pennock; first baseman Lou Gehrig; second baseman Tony Lazzeri; third baseman Joe Sewell; and catcher Bill Dickey. It was a team that compared favorably to the 1927 Yankees, which is often considered the greatest team of all time. The Cubs simply didn't stand a chance.

The Yankees won the first two games of the Series fairly easily, 12–6 and 5–2. In game three, with the score tied at 4–4 in the fifth, Ruth came to bat. He had already smacked a homer in the first inning, and the Cubs and their fans were heckling him, calling the Babe fat, old, and an "ape." Ruth grinned and took a Charlie Root pitch for strike one. The noise level increased.

Root fired another pitch past Ruth for strike two. More howling. Ruth stepped out of the batters box and pointed somewhere—some thought to the Cubs dugout, some thought toward pitcher Root, some thought toward the center field bleachers where he planned to hit it. Then he stepped back into the box. Root tried to sneak a fastball past Ruth. The Babe golfed it over the center-field fence, laughing as he rounded the bases. The Yankees went on to win the game, 7–5, and wrapped up the Series the next day.

It was Babe Ruth's most famous home run and is still hotly debated by sportswriters as to whether he called it ahead of time. Surely, he must have called it, right?

Ruth, a good-natured soul, didn't disagree. Root, who tended not to worry about those kinds of things (the team lost; who cares what Ruth did or didn't do?) would never correct a sportswriter who brought up the story.

The Cubs went to the World Series again in 1935, only to lose to the Detroit Tigers. They'd get another chance at the most coveted title in 1938, but this time their opponent was even more formidable than the Tigers. This time, they had to face the New York Yankees, who only seemed to be getting better. Babe Ruth was gone, but a young center fielder by the name of Joe DiMaggio was now the team's star. It was really the pitching and defense that won this Series, though, as pitchers Red Ruffing, with two complete-game wins, and Monte Pearson, with one, were the key performers. The Cubs were unable to match up with the Yankees, who swept all four games to win their third straight championship.

No one knew it at the time, but it was the beginning of the end for this franchise. The Cubs would have a few good years over the next six decades, but they would also have many more bad ones. Still, while there was talk of frustrating defeats and laments in the sports columns about the hard-luck Cubs, there was still optimism. The team seemed to be heading in the right direction—but it wasn't.

A Wrong Turn: The 1940s

P. K. Wrigley was an excellent businessman, but he was not necessarily a good ball-club owner. To save money, he cut back on the team's farm system and scouting staff. That, in itself, was the biggest blow to the Cubs, as they were no longer able to draw on new blood from within the organization. The club was more reliant on acquiring players from other organizations, which was always an iffy and expensive proposition; when a club has to trade for talent, it inevitably gives something up. While teams like the Yankees and St. Louis Cardinals fleshed out their teams with players they had signed and brought up through their respective minor league networks, the Cubs often had to look elsewhere.

During the first part of the 1940s, the Cubs floundered, finishing no higher than fifth from 1940 to 1943 and fourth in 1944. But in 1945, the Cubs received some help as a result of World War II. A number of

National League stars were drafted, but most of the Cub regulars were too old. The Cubs had a good pitching staff led by Hal Wyse and Claude Passeau, a solid infield led by Phil Cavarretta at first and Stan Hack at third, and a strong outfield led by Andy Pafko in center. Chicago won ninety-eight games to finish three games ahead of the Cardinals, who were sorely missing Stan Musial that season.

They would once again face the Tigers in the World Series, and no one was predicting a sure winner. That is, no one except the owner of the Billy Goat Tavern.

William "Billy Goat" Sianis, tavern owner and goat lover, arrived at Wrigley to watch game four with his beloved goat, Murphy, in tow. When the goat was turned away (apparently, farm animals are a distraction), Sianis cursed the team and the ballpark, saying they'd never win a Series until the goat got in. The gatekeeper should have listened to the goat keeper.

Chicago took games one

and three thanks to solid pitching from Passeau and Hank Borowy, a veteran the Cubs had snatched away from the Yankees. Due to wartime gasoline restrictions, the first three games were played in Detroit and the final four games were scheduled to be in Chicago. Up two games to one and going home for the next four games, the Cubs only needed to split the remaining games at home to win it all.

The Tigers won the next two games. Pitcher Dizzy Trout's five-hitter

in the fourth game tied the series at two games apiece, and Detroit's future Hall of Famer Hank Greenberg stroked three doubles to key an 8–4 Tiger win in the fifth tilt.

Game six was a wild affair that saw Stan Hack drill a double past Big Hank Greenberg to drive in the winning run in the tenth inning for an 8–7 final. The concluding game of the Series found Grimm, who had used four pitchers in the previous game, without a starter. Borowy, who had won two games already, volunteered to go in. He had pitched four innings in relief two days prior but declared himself fit.

He wasn't. The Tigers pounded Borowy, who didn't get an out in the first inning. By then, a stunned Cubs crowd watched as Detroit waltzed to an easy 9–3 win.

If one could pinpoint the moment when optimism began draining out of many Cubs fans, one might be tempted to put a marker on this game. The team had played well, fought valiantly, and lost ignobly. There would be some close playoff calls in the next sixty years, but not another World Series. Some may blame pitching, others coaching, but there are many who blame the banning of the goat.

The rest of the decade was less than noteworthy. The Cubs finished third in 1946, sixth in 1947, and dead last in 1948 and 1949. In 1950, they were seventh.

Bright Spot Banks: The 1950s

If the 1940s were a struggle, the 1950s were worse. The Cubs lost ninety or more games four times in the decade and never finished higher than fifth. Their 77–77 record in 1952 was the only time the team would finish at .500 or better in the decade.

There was only one consolation. In 1953, the Cubs brought up a lanky, power-hitting shortstop named Ernie Banks. Banks, a black man who was much smarter than sportswriters ever gave him credit for, would help to reshape the racial profile of the city of Chicago.

Banks was not the only black player promoted by the Cubs. In fact, he was originally brought up to keep another black player, Eugene Baker, company on the road. But he quickly took over as the team's best player, hitting .314 in limited action that season.

Although the Brooklyn Dodgers' Jackie Robinson had integrated baseball in 1947, most big league teams were still uncomfortable signing and playing blacks. The usual practice in the 1950s, and, for some teams, even into the late 1960s, was to sign an even number of black players, either two or four, so that white teammates would not have to share a hotel room with them.

In 1954, Banks was the regular starter, hitting .275 with nineteen home runs and 79 RBI. By the next season, Banks was one of the best

players in baseball, winning the MVP award in 1958 and 1959. It was the first time in baseball history that a player from a last-place team won that award. Andre Dawson would match the feat . . . also while playing for the Cubs.

Banks was the one bright spot for the moribund Cubs teams of the 1950s. And more than his talent, his good nature contributed to his popularity. His cry of "Let's play two!" perfectly evoked his kidlike enthusiasm for the game. Even in an era long before the huge salaries of today, baseball players were still professionals and complained about various little inanities. But Banks's sunny optimism—no mean thing given the lousy teams he played on in Chicago— marked him as a hero in baseball as much as his offensive output. While his enthusiasm was deemed a little disingenuous by some of his teammates, for Banks, who was born impoverished and raised in an oppressively racist climate in Texas, playing baseball for a living was heaven.

For those white fans who, due to segregation and strong racist stereotypes that dominated society in those days, primarily perceived blacks as a surly, lazy bunch, Banks was a revelation. He played hard, he clearly loved the game, and he was darn good. He made it easy for Cubs fans to root for a black man. It is no exaggeration to say that Ernie Banks paved the way for many black ballplayers in Chicago.

The Road to the Right Track: The 1960s

The early 1960s continued to be a letdown for Cubs fans. Back-to-back ninety-loss seasons in 1960 and 1961 were followed by 103 defeats in 1962. Outfielder Billy Williams was promoted from the minors in 1959, and third baseman Ron Santo came up in 1960, but those two stars weren't nearly enough to pull the Cubs out of their tailspin.

Part of the problem was "the College." The College of Coaches was a new idea of Wrigley's that he established in 1961. The concept wasn't bad, but the reality was devastating. The idea was to rotate several coaches throughout the minors and up to the Cubs on a regular basis, ensuring that all future coaches would learn "Cub baseball" and be on the same page.

The biggest problem, according to many players, was consistency, the very quality the College aspired to. In his autobiography, Cub great Ron Santo pointed out that he would often get different tips on ways to hit and field from different managers. As a young player, Santo wanted to develop his skills. "But getting different instructions from different managers was driving me crazy," he admitted in his book.

Santo was evidently not alone. From 1961 to 1964, the Cubs never finished higher than seventh.

The College of Coaches was mercifully closed down in 1962, although team leader Bob Kennedy's official title was still "head coach" instead of "manager." Wrigley, by now smarting from two decades of being beaten up in the media for being a loser, went out and hired a winner. In 1965, he signed Leo "the Lip" Durocher, a cocky, caustic, and canny skipper. He had won pennants with Brooklyn in 1941 and with the New York Giants in 1951 and 1954. He was known for his knowledge of the game and for his sarcastic manner with owners, sportswriters, and some of his players.

Chicago sportswriters couldn't believe it. After years of hiring former players, it seemed as though the Cubs were finally heading in the right direction. It didn't happen overnight, but the Cubs began getting better ballplayers. Over the next few years, they traded for pitchers Ferguson Jenkins and Bill Hands, and catcher Randy Hundley. They also brought up second baseman Glenn Beckert, shortstop Don Kessinger, and pitcher Kenny Holtzman.

These new players, coupled with regulars Williams, Banks, and Santo, brought energy to the Cubs, and the team began to jell.

It didn't all happen overnight. The team had finished eighth in 1965.

At a press conference prior to the start of the 1966 season, Durocher confidently predicted that "this team is not an eighth-place team." They weren't. The Cubs finished tenth, losing 103 games.

But the players, even at that point, believed they were on the right track. For example, Durocher understood that a youngster named Glenn Beckert clearly did not have the arm to play shortstop. He moved Beckert to second base, where he played for nine years.

The Cubs were also not afraid to make trades. They traded Larry Jackson and Bob Buhl, two veteran pitchers, to the Phillies for outfielder Adolfo Phillips and a virtually unknown pitcher, Ferguson Jenkins. The Chicago press was dubious, particularly in Jenkins's case. But Jenkins went on to win twenty or more games from 1967 to 1972 for Chicago. Another great pick was Randy Hundley, a languishing catcher Chicago snagged from the Giants and who, under the care of the Cubs, became one of the majors' best catchers for several years.

In 1969, Chicago went 11–1 to start the season. The pitching was superb, the hitting exceptional. On August 19, Holtzman tossed a no-hitter against the Atlanta Braves, winning 3–0. The Cubs were eight games ahead of the New York Mets. It looked good.

But suddenly, it wasn't. The Cubs stopped hitting, and the Mets, who had a solid pitching staff led by Tom Seaver, Jerry Koosman, and a young Nolan Ryan, sprinted past them to win the pennant.

Cubs fans blamed Durocher for playing his regulars too much (in particular Hundley, who wound up playing in games even when Durocher had given him the day off) and burning them out down the stretch. In reality, the Cubs had a great starting lineup but not a lot of depth on the bench. Leo the Lip had to play the starters—he lost too much in his lineup when he didn't.

Years later, people would point to the Cubs' collapse as yet another in a decades-long series of disappointments, an example of how the Cubs always managed to come from ahead to lose. Was the goat still kicking in '69? As we'll see as the decades move on, that goat had a lot of kids.

Sutter's Suitors: The 1970s

The 1970s may have been even more frustrating than the 1960s. After a second-place finish in 1972, the Cubs finished between third and sixth over the next eleven years. They were consistently bad, not posting a single winning record during that period. Durocher

was replaced by Whitey Lockman in 1972, and the team seemed intent on getting rid of many of the Cub icons of the late 1960s and early 1970s. In 1974, Jenkins was traded to Texas, Beckert to San Diego, and Hundley to Minnesota. Williams went to Oakland in 1975. The team didn't improve.

The Cubs did have a few bright spots. Bill Madlock came to Chicago in the Jenkins deal. Madlock had a powerful, compact swing that enabled him to spray hits all over Wrigley. In 1975, he belted 182 hits for a league-leading .354 average that was the fifteenth-best mark in Cub history, and the best since Phil Cavarretta's .355 in 1945.

In the ninth inning of the All-Star Game that season, Madlock drilled a two-run single to win the game and share in the MVP honors, the first Cub to earn the honor.

Madlock, nicknamed "Mad Dog" because of his intense play, dropped off slightly in 1976, but his .339 average was once again a league best. Madlock became the first—and to date only—Cub to win back-to-back batting crowns.

The other player of note who came to Chicago in 1976 was reliever Bruce Sutter. In 1973, as a twenty-year-old minor league, Sutter suffered a serious elbow injury that nearly ended his career. But he rehabbed his arm and, with the help of roving pitching instructor Fred Martin and Cubs pitching coach Mike Rourke, developed a split-fingered fastball that he could make dig sharply downward as it reached the plate. Sutter had something of a genetic advantage here: his fingers were unusually long, and he could curl them almost completely around the ball when he threw.

Sutter was called up to the majors in 1976 and saved ten games that season. By 1977, he was the Cubs' closer, one of the best in the league. He saved 31, 27, 37, and 28 games over the next four years for Chicago. These seem like modest totals, but Sutter averaged one and two-thirds innings per appearance in that span, as opposed to closers today, who rarely work more than an inning.

In April of 1977, Philip K. Wrigley died, and his son William Wrigley took over. William was also a pretty sharp businessman, but things were happening outside of Chicago that would conspire against the Wrigley family. Free agency had come to baseball with a vengeance, and the Cubs struggled to compete. In 1980, Sutter's contract was up, and he requested a huge raise that would put his salary at $700,000, a number that would have made him one of the highest-paid pitchers in the game. Wrigley balked and traded him to the St. Louis Cardinals. In 1982, the Cards would win the World Championship, with Sutter a key cog in their indomitable machine.

The Coming of the Trib: The 1980s

Following the 1982 season, Wrigley sold the Cubs to the Chicago Tribune Corporation for $20.5 million, ending the family's sixty-three-year ownership of the franchise. Corporate ownership was not something many Cubs fans looked forward to, but they had little choice.

"The Trib," as it is known by locals, proved more consistent than the Wrigleys. It went out and hired Dallas Green as general manager in October 1981 and gave him a mandate—and the money—to improve the

club. Green traded for second baseman Ryne Sandberg, traded for two ex-Dodgers, Bill Buckner and Ron Cey, and improved the pitching staff.

By 1984, the Cubs were contenders again. By early June, Green realized he needed one more pitcher and picked up veteran Rick Sutcliffe. Sutcliffe went 16–1 with the Cubs, and Chicago won the National League East crown in 1984. The fans were ecstatic. Unlike 1969, this team had not faded.

Their opponents in the National League Championship Series (the two leagues had split into Eastern and Western divisions in 1969) were the San Diego Padres, an interesting collection of veterans, including ex-Dodger Steve Garvey and ex-Yankees Graig Nettles and Goose Gossage, and young bucks like Alan Wiggins and Tony Gwynn. Cubs fans were confident but cautious.

Emotions were running high after Sutcliffe dominated the Padres in game one, 13–0, and pitcher Steve Trout picked up a 4–2 win in game two of the best-of-five series. The Padres never panicked, though. The two teams went back to San Diego, and the Padres won the third game, 7–1. In game four, a home run by Garvey in the bottom of the ninth gave San Diego a 7–5 win that tied the series.

Still, the Cubs had Sutcliffe going in the finale. The Cubs jumped out to a 3–0 lead after two innings, but the Padres kept their cool. They scored two runs in the sixth inning and exploded for four more in the seventh to chase Sutcliffe. And in the eighth, the best closer of the late 1970s and early 1980s, Gossage, took the mound and shut the door on Chicago once again.

The Cubs had had it in their grasp. They won the first two games of the series. They had to win one of the next three. And they blew it. As usual, said their fans. Been there, done that. And would do it again . . .

Sosa's Team: The 1990s

The nineties proved a mostly cruel decade for the Cubs, with six losing seasons in the eight years from 1990 to 1997, as a lack of depth and pitching continued to plague the team.

The 1998 season was a different story. Outfielder Sammy Sosa, acquired from the White Sox in 1992, was the reason.

The player who would become a fan favorite in the late 1990s didn't have a great beginning with the Cubs. In his first few years with the team, Sosa

struck out too much and looked awkward at the plate. But in 1994, Sosa hit .300, slugged .545, and even stole twenty-two bases. In 1995, Sosa was named to the All-Star team, hit thirty-six homers, and drove in 119 runs. He also stole thirty-four bases that year, making him only the second Cub besides Ryne Sandberg to lead the team in stolen bases and home runs for three years. Perhaps more importantly, Sosa played hard and clearly enjoyed the game. His combination of talent and hustle made him adored by fans of the Cubs and admired by fans of baseball.

By 1998, Sosa had put it all together, stroking a team-record sixty-six home runs and carrying on a season-long race with the St. Louis Cardinals' Mark McGwire for the home-run title.

For more than three months, America turned its lonely baseball eyes to Sammy and Big Mac. Their home-run race exploded out of the sports page to grace the national news scene. As both raced toward Roger Maris's record of sixty-one faster than the El around the Loop, it became more than just a race to see who would break the record, it became a living, breathing resuscitation of the national pastime, still reeling from a disastrous strike four years earlier. Thanks to Sammy and Mac and their sportsmanlike approach to what could have been a rancorous battle (the Cubs and Cardinals have been bitter enemies for decades), baseball blossomed.

Homer for homer, tater for tater, they matched each other until McGwire pulled ahead in September. He became the first to sixty-two early in the month. Sammy matched him soon after, but there was no silver medal for second place. Sammy took the lead in the race for about forty-five minutes, but the new record would go to whoever finished with more on the season. Sammy's sixty-six fell short; Big Mac slugged five on the final weekend to reach seventy. Everyone took a deep breath, but everyone knew then (the real big steroids scandal was years away) that baseball was back.

McGwire's seventy homers won the battle, but Sosa, with a league-leading 158 RBI and 134 runs scored, drove his team into the playoffs and won the MVP award. The Cubs beat the San Francisco Giants in a one-game playoff for the wild card slot but were eliminated by the Braves in the first round. The playoffs had expanded from two to four teams in both leagues, and a third tier of playoffs, the Division Series, was added. Thanks to Sammy, the Cubs had made it to the playoffs. But then they lost—what else is new?

A New Millennium: 2000 and Beyond

The Cubs struggled from 1999 to 2001 despite Sosa's sixty-three, fifty, and sixty-four home runs, respectively, in those three seasons, making him the only player to hit sixty or more home runs three times in a career.

In 2003, Chicago reached the playoffs again behind Sosa, fireballer Kerry Wood, Moises Alou, and another young pitching phenom, Mark Prior. The Cubs, with Wood winning two games and Prior the other, knocked out the Braves in the Division Series, 3–2. It was the first playoff series the Cubs had won since winning the World Series in 1908.

In the National League Championship Series, the Cubs faced the Florida Marlins, who were enjoying only the second winning season in their short history.

The Cubs took a 3–1 lead in the series as Aramis Ramirez and Alex Gonzalez each belted three homers in the first four games. Josh Beckett threw a two-hit shutout in game five for a 4–0 Marlins win. Then came game six.

Prior was cruising in Wrigley, leading 3–0. Then the Marlins started to hit. They scored eight runs in the eighth inning and won the game, 8–3.

What happened was a complete collapse. With one out in the inning, left fielder Moises Alou was chasing a pop fly that was slowly drifting toward the stands. Alou stuck out his glove, and Cubs fan Steve Bartman stuck out his. Bartman deflected the ball, and Alou failed to get it. Alou glared at Bartman, and as the runs piled up in the inning, the fans began getting restless. Bartman, a twenty-six-year-old youth coach, had to be escorted out of the park by police. He watched game seven under protective guard at his house.

It was a stunning disintegration, although fan interference was not a factor. The pop-up Alou chased was in the stands, not on the playing field, and under baseball's rules Bartman had every right to go after the ball. The real reason for the Cubs' loss was the implosion of the pitching staff, and a key error by Gonzalez that extended the inning. Even though

The most infamous foul ball in Cubs history. Moises Alou duels with Cub fan Steve Bartman in the eighth inning of game six of the 2003 NLCS.

the Cubs had Wood on the mound in game seven, it seemed a foregone conclusion that the Cubs would not, could not, win the game. The Marlins jumped out to a 3–0 lead and won the National League pennant, 9–6.

As in 1945, 1969, 1984, and 1989, the Cubs found a way to lose. Perhaps more than any other incident in their long and checkered history, the Bartman Game, as it came to be known, symbolized the Cubs' status as the team that just couldn't get it done. When the similarly long-cursed Boston Red Sox won it all in 2004 and then their crosstown rivals in futility, the White Sox, became champs in 2005, the Cubs stood alone atop the pantheon of nonwinners. But did their fans jump ship? Was a ticket at Wrigley suddenly easy to get? Was the beer warm? No, sir, no, the fans just kept coming to cheer on their beloved Cubs.

The long and winding road continues. The goal remains the same for the Cubs and whomever owns them or plays for them: win a World Series. For their fans, however, it's a different story. The Cubs' long record of heartbreak has created a sort of Zen-like calm amid the faithful who have come to understand that with this team, it's not the destination (though Wrigley is a nice destination)—it's the journey. Next stop, 1060 West Addison; we'll save you a seat. ★

The Chicago White Sox ★ ★ ★

Up until 2005, you'd have been forgiven if you'd had to stop and think about what the "other" team in Chicago was called. Everyone knows about the Cubs. Those who aren't baseball fans know about the Cubs. Presidents knew the Cubs—heck, one commander in chief even *broadcast* them at one point (see page 159). But that other team, they're the, um, let's see . . .

Oh, yeah, they're the World Champions!

No longer the second team in the Second City, the Chicago White Sox wrote perhaps the greatest chapter in their long history when they swept the Houston Astros to win the 2005 World Series. In so doing, they broke a championship-free streak that stretched back to 1917. No longer were they the team that had "thrown a World Series since they won one" (see the 1919 Black Sox, page 52). No longer were they second fiddle to the uptown Cubs. And what's perhaps just as sweet, they left the Cubs behind as the last original Major League team without a World Series title since 1908. Take that, you Wrigley Bleacher Bums!

The White Sox of 2005 followed some story lines that had nice tendrils back to their earlier days. They won the 1906 World Series as the "Hitless Wonders"; the 2005 team was not exactly hitless, but they weren't an offensive juggernaut either. They won the 1959 American League pennant as the "Go-Go Sox," stealing more bases than they hit homers; in 2005, breaking with typical American League play, the Sox played "small ball" all the way to the title. In winning, they put some of the shame of the 1919 Series in the past; no club carried a heavier burden of baseball pain than that caused by those Black Sox, but 2005 put that event in the background again.

The story of the White Sox, then, is basically one of success, a century of not very good news, and then the best news of all at the end. The stuff in between had some pretty good entertainment value, though, from the Comiskey family's exploits as owners, to those exciting Go-Go Sox, to the truly bizarre exploits of promotional wizard Bill Veeck in the 1970s (can you say baseball shorts and fans run amok?). Throughout the twentieth century, the White Sox remained in the shadow of the Cubs, existing as perhaps the most obscure of the original big-league teams. But that changed in 2005, for the better. Strap on your batting helmets for a bumpy ride, but you'll enjoy the soft landing.

A Team Grows in Iowa: The Late 1800s

The Chicago White Sox have roots dating back to 1894, miles away from the Windy City—in Sioux City, Iowa. The team began as charter members of Ban Johnson's Western League, considered a minor league at the time. Johnson had previously worked as a sportswriter for the *Cincinnati Commercial Gazette* but was attracted to the challenge of running the foundering minor-league operation.

Charlie Comiskey, a former first baseman with the Cincinnati Reds, purchased the Sioux City franchise after the 1894 season and immediately moved it to St. Paul, Minnesota. Comiskey had had a thirteen-year career in the American Association, National League, and Players' League before retiring as a player and bringing his managerial skills into the game. In later years, sportswriters dubbed Comiskey "the Old Roman" due to his regal bearing, but in those early days his cunning equated him more with Machiavelli. With the savvy Comiskey and determined Johnson holding the reins of the Western League, it quickly became one of the best-run operations in the country. Payrolls and schedules were met, well-respected umpires were hired, and the quality of play was just below major-league level.

Johnson believed the Western League teams were as good as any in the National League and schemed to raise his boys up to go head-to-head with the majors. One of his principal cohorts was Comiskey.

As the plotting progressed, Comiskey spoke to Al Spalding, manager of the National League Cubs, who were then known as the Orphans. Comiskey told Spalding he wanted to found a minor-league franchise on the South Side of Chicago, starting with the 1900 season. Spalding's team, located on the North Side, wasn't too worried. The minors were the *minors*, after all—what threat could they pose? Perhaps Spalding should have paid closer attention.

Comiskey was as good as his word and moved his St. Paul franchise to Chicago that year. The Old Roman then issued a further threat to Spalding by appropriating the National League team's name, calling his team the Chicago White Stockings. "Stockings" was shortened to "Sox" within a couple of years, as it was a better fit for newspaper headlines; even in the early years, the Old Roman was determined his team would make headlines frequently. That settled, he put his boys to work in South Side Park, a former cricket field.

A New League in Town: The 1900s

As Comiskey worked his magic in Chicago, Johnson kept busy, too. In 1900, Johnson changed the name of his Western League to the American League and announced its teams would soon rival the National League in quality. National League owners scoffed at this new league's ambitions, but Johnson was not bluffing. He encouraged the eight American League franchises to raid the National League for players, which those teams gladly did. In 1901, with those star players in hand, the American League became a major league. Eight cities were home to new American League franchises that first season: Chicago, Boston, Detroit, Philadelphia, Baltimore, Washington, Cleveland, and Milwaukee. Three of the franchises—in Boston, Philadelphia, and Chicago—competed directly with National League teams in their home city.

The White Sox scored an enormous coup by signing pitcher Clark Griffith prior to the 1901 season. Griffith, formerly the property of the Cubs, became not only the best pitcher on the White Sox roster but also the manager of the team. Comiskey also signed pitcher Nixey Callahan and second baseman Sam Mertes away from the Cubs, right fielder Fielder Jones from Brooklyn, and, a year earlier, center fielder Dummy Hoy from Louisville. Spalding's team suddenly had reason to take notice of their talented neighbors.

That lineup gave the White Sox the 1901 American League pennant, as Griffith won twenty-four games that season for the 83–53 team. The White Sox also led the American League in attendance that year, attracting 354,350 fans. The Cubs were sixth in the National

League but only drew 205,071 spectators. In Chicago, at least, the American League was a huge success.

Griffith spent less time on the mound in 1902 and eventually left the team in 1903 to take the reins of the American League franchise in New York City. The White Sox fell back for a few years.

Comiskey was undaunted and spent 1904 and 1905 retooling the squad. He wanted a team built on pitching and speed and to that end began acquiring a stable of good hurlers. By 1906, the pitching staff was a monster: twenty-game winners Frank Owen (22–13) and Nick

Altrock (20–13); lefty Doc White (18–6), whose 1.52 ERA was the lowest in the league; and up-and-coming star Ed Walsh (17–13).

But it's more than a pitching game, and the White Sox had very few hitters on that 1906 squad. Their best batsman was veteran shortstop George Davis, who batted .277 and was the leading RBI man with 80. But they allowed the fewest runs in the league (460), were third in the league in stolen bases with 214, and their thirty-two shutouts were tops in the majors. They were dubbed "the Hitless Wonders" and ended dead last in league batting with a

.230 mark. However, this nickname was a misnomer. Despite their low batting average, the White Sox were an above-average offensive team, finishing third in the league in runs scored despite playing in baseball's toughest park for hitters.

The Sox, under player-manager Fielder Jones, won ninety-three games and claimed the pennant by three. They were the masters of the bunt, the hit-and-run, the stolen base, and the sacrifice fly. Few teams, if any, could manufacture runs better than the 1906 White Sox.

Their opponent in the World Series would be none other than their crosstown rivals, the Cubs. The Cubs, in contrast to the White Sox, had a plethora of solid hitters, including third baseman Harry Steinfeldt, the league leader in RBI (83) and hits (174). First baseman and manager Frank Chance, christened "the Peerless Leader" by the press for his toughness, led the league in stolen bases (57) and runs scored (103).

The National League champions hadn't developed one area at the expense of another like the Sox had; they were flush with starting pitchers: Mordecai "Three Finger" Brown won twenty-six games for the team and led the league with a 1.04 ERA, Jack Pfeister was 20–8, and Ed Reulbach was 19–4.

As if that weren't enough, the National Leaguers also had the immortal defensive tandem of Chance at first, Johnny Evers at second, and Joe Tinker at shortstop. They went 116–36, and those 116 wins are still a National League record. Given the team's strong infield, need it be said? The White Sox were huge underdogs entering the Series.

The First Battle for Chicago: The 1906 World Series

Game one of the 1906 World Series took place during a light snowfall on the West Side Grounds, the Cubs' home field. Altrock and Brown matched four-hitters, but the difference in the 2–1 White Sox win was an RBI single by Isbell in the sixth to give the visitors a 2–0 lead. The home team scored one run in the bottom of the inning, but that was it.

Game two, played at South Side Park, saw Reulbach fire a one-hitter as the National League champions romped, 7–1, to tie the series. But the White Sox responded by winning their second road game of the series, 3–0, behind Walsh's two-hit shutout. Utility infielder George Rohe, playing third base for the injured Lee Tannehill, belted a three-run triple in the sixth inning to score all the runs in the game. It was Rohe's second career triple. He would hit two more in his four-year career.

But again, the National Leaguers battled back behind Brown. The best pitcher in the National League beat Altrock 1–0, firing a two-hitter in game four. The series was tied, but fans sensed the momentum shifting to the underdog White Sox, who had managed six runs in the first four games but were still tied.

In game five, the White Sox fell behind 3–1 in the first inning, rallied to tie the game in the third, and exploded with a four-run fourth inning. Isbell ripped a World Series–record four doubles in the game, scored two runs, and drove in two more. The Sox won, 8–6. For the first time in the series, a pitching staff member had choked, and he belonged, unexpectedly, to the favored National Leaguers.

With his team on the brink of elimination, a nervous Chance put Brown back on the mound after only one day's rest. The future Hall of Famer didn't have it, though, and the Sox scored three runs in the first inning and four in the second. White Sox pitcher Doc White was superb, going the distance and scattering seven hits in an easy 8–3 win.

The upset stunned the National League champions, many of whom had bet heavily on themselves to win. As for the White Sox, Comiskey gave manager Fielder Jones a check for $15,000 and told him to split it up among the team. But their euphoria over the victory and Comiskey's generosity was short-lived.

At first the players were grateful for this gesture by the Old Roman until they found out that the money represented raises he had planned for the team the next year. This incident proved to be a dark omen of Comiskey's financial shenanigans down the road.

A Rebuilding and a New Building: The 1910s

In 1910, Comiskey unveiled a new South Side stadium called Comiskey Park. His star player, pitcher Big Ed Walsh, was invited to

help design the field. Given his position on the field, Walsh lobbied for a large, cavernous park with lots of foul territory. It was understandable that Big Ed would want to promote and implement such a design, but as a result, the park's large open spaces, while advantageous to a pitcher, were not necessarily a favorite for hitters. The stadium's design would ultimately affect the team's play for decades to come.

Despite the new stadium, the White Sox were still slogging around in the "second division," the name sportswriters had given to the teams in the bottom half of the standings. Comiskey wanted to improve his roster, and in 1912, he picked up pitcher Eddie Cicotte from the pitching-rich Boston Red Sox. In 1915, Comiskey purchased a future Hall of Famer, second baseman Eddie Collins, from the Philadelphia Athletics for $50,000, and then traded three minor players along with $31,500 in cash to pick up the best hitter in the majors, "Shoeless" Joe Jackson.

These men were the key to the Sox' resurgence. They were also a part of the reason the team crashed and burned; in 1919, those players would be part of the infamous squad known as the Chicago Black Sox.

1917: World Champs Again

In the years before the scandal, there was calm. In 1917, the infield was solid with third baseman Buck Weaver, shortstop Swede Risberg, second baseman Eddie Collins, and first baseman Chick Gandil. Joining Jackson in the outfield were Nemo Leibold and Happy Felsch, with reserve outfielder John "Shano" Collins providing depth. Cicotte, Urban "Red" Faber, and Claude "Lefty" Williams anchored the pitching staff, while the catcher was future Hall of Famer Ray Schalk.

The White Sox took over first place that July and steadily built their lead on the defending World Champion Red Sox. Even a solid year by Boston's big left-handed pitching star, Babe Ruth, could not keep the Red Sox in contention. Chicago won a hundred games for the first time in franchise history and won the pennant by nine games.

The Sox were a slight favorite over the National League champion New York Giants, who were led by left fielder George Burns and third baseman Heinie Zimmerman. The pitching staff was headed by Ferdinand "Ferdie" Schupp, who won twenty-one of his sixty-one career victories in 1917 to lead the Giants. Managing the New Yorkers was the fiery John "Muggsy" McGraw, but this was not to be one of McGraw's better pennant teams.

The White Sox, behind Cicotte's seven-hitter, took the first game at home, 2–1, as Shano Collins rapped three hits. Red Faber won game two, 7–2, scattering eight hits. The two teams moved to New York for games three and four, and the Giants evened the series with a pair of wins.

Back in Comiskey Park on October 13 for game five, Eddie Collins's RBI single was the key hit in a three-run eighth inning that gave Chicago an 8–5 win. Faber was the winning pitcher with two innings of shutout relief.

Then, on October 15, the Sox took care of business. Faber took the mound as the starter and fired a six-hitter to close out the Giants, 4–2. Eddie Collins had hit .409, stolen three bases, and scored four runs. Weaver had hit .333 and Jackson .304. Faber had won three

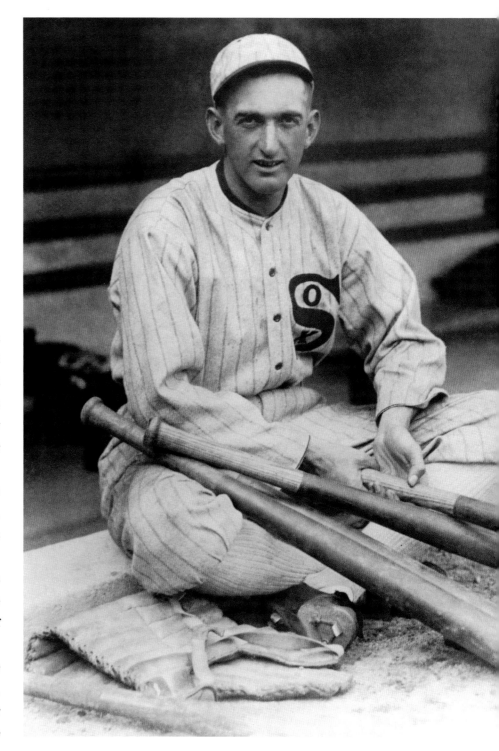

games, tying a World Series record. The White Sox had won their second World Championship.

Ironically, years later, McGraw would confide to several friends that he thought his second baseman, Buck Herzog, had played so poorly that he might have bet against his own team. But who would do such a thing?

The Chicago Black Sox of 1919

World War I decimated the White Sox as Jackson, Collins, Faber, and Risberg, among others, were drafted into service and were lost to the team for parts of 1918. Chicago finished sixth, but by 1919 the war was over and the White Sox were back.

Once again, the Sox took over first place in July and never looked back, winning eighty-eight games in a shortened 140-game season to finish just ahead of the Cleveland Indians.

The White Sox were favored to win their second World Championship in three years. They faced a Cincinnati Reds team that was talented but not an even match for the skill of Chicago's players.

In 1919, though, talent and skill wouldn't be the decisive factors in the matchup; rather, the championship would come down to something much more sinister.

Comiskey, revered by the fans and sportswriters, knew which side his bread was buttered on. He lavished the local sportswriters with food and booze. In turn, the sportswriters portrayed Comiskey as a wealthy but generous owner who treated his players like sons.

In truth, Comiskey was a cheapskate. The league recommended $4 a day for meals. The Old Roman gave his boys $3, and charged his players fifty cents a day to clean their uniforms. When recalcitrant White Sox players began wearing their uniforms dirty, Comiskey ordered that they be cleaned and docked his players for it.

That was a big deal for players whose earnings were some of the lowest in baseball. Star hitter Jackson was making $6,000, and many other teammates were in the $3,000 to $4,000 range. Only Collins, at $15,000, was being paid a salary comparable to players on other teams in the league. Comiskey was so ashamed of Jackson's meager salary that he told reporters that Joe was making $10,000. Jackson was so embarrassed that he didn't bother to refute Comiskey's claims.

Worse, the Sox were one of the best-drawing teams in either league, a fact the papers continually trumpeted. Charlie Comiskey was clearly making money on the White Sox—a lot of money. The only problem: his players were not sharing in the bounty.

So, it was in this climate, in mid-September in Boston, just before the 1919 World Series began, that gamblers approached several members of the White Sox with an offer of $10,000 apiece to play just well enough to lose the Series. The White Sox eventually struck deals with two separate gambling syndicates, one for a total of $80,000 and the other for $100,000.

A total of eight players were reportedly in on the fix: Jackson, Weaver, Felsch, Gandil, Risberg, Williams, Cicotte, and utility infielder Fred McMullin. Jackson insisted he never attended any of the alleged meetings with gamblers, a point the other players did not dispute. Jackson also asserted that he was asked by Gandil twice to participate in the fix and told him that he would not. Gandil's response to Jackson was allegedly, "The thing is going forward, Joe. You might as well be in on it."

Just before the start of the Series, Jackson went to Sox manager "Kid" Gleason and asked out of the game, claiming illness. Gleason passed it off as nerves and insisted that Jackson play.

Pitch one, game one of this best-of-nine series: Cicotte, a control pitcher who only hit two batters during the entire regular season, nailed Reds leadoff hitter Maurice Rath right between the shoulder blades. Allegedly, this misfire was a signal to gamblers that the plot was going forward.

The Reds would ice the game with a five-run fourth, and Cicotte would last only 3²/3 innings. Earle "Greasy" Neale, the future football Hall of Famer, stroked three hits in the win.

Although that was the worst Cicotte had looked in months, the White Sox (or at least, the honest ones) were still confident after the first game. The team's other ace, Lefty Williams, was pitching game two for the Sox. The Reds countered with thirty-five-year-old "Slim" Sallee, a solid pitcher.

In the fourth inning, Lefty, who had walked only fifty-eight men all year, blew up. He walked three batters and gave up three runs in the inning. The Sox outhit the Reds, 10–4, but still lost, 4–2.

By this time, some of the players who had not been in on the fix knew something was up. Catcher Ray Schalk was so infuriated by Williams, who had shaken him off throughout the game, that he confronted his teammate outside the clubhouse and struck him.

The games shifted to Chicago, and the Sox had rookie Dickie Kerr pitching. Kerr threw a three-hit shutout, and the Sox won, 3–0, as Gandil's single drove in Jackson and Felsch. Jackson, with two singles in the game, was now hitting .455 for the series.

Game four saw another uncharacteristically sloppy performance by Cicotte, who made two errors in the fifth inning, which allowed two Cincinnati runs to score. They were the only runs of the game, as the Reds won, 2–0, to take a commanding 3–1 lead in the World Series.

By now, Gleason was sure something was up. At one point, he declined to name his starter, although it was clearly Williams's turn. Eventually, Gleason put Williams on the mound, and the pitcher responded with a four-hitter. The trouble was, the Reds' Hod Eller fired a three-hitter. An error by Felsch in the sixth helped the Reds score four runs, and they eventually won, 5–0.

Had this World Series been played under the previous year's rules, the Cincinnati Reds would have been World Champions, winning four of the five games. With the new extended series, however, the Reds still had to win one more, and Gleason asserted that his club would not go down without a fight.

Once again, the rookie Kerr, a former bantamweight boxer, got the call. And once again, Kerr came through, going the distance in a ten-inning game, scattering eleven hits and winning, 5–4. The Sox trailed 4–0 before rallying with a run in the fifth and three in the sixth. In the tenth inning, Jackson bunted Weaver over to third. Gandil's RBI single scored Weaver, and Kerr held on in the bottom of the inning for the victory.

Gleason went with Cicotte in game seven, and this time, Eddie pitched superbly, firing a seven-hitter for a 4–1 win. Once again, Jackson drilled an RBI single to score Shano Collins.

Suddenly, the momentum seemed to be swinging back Chicago's way. If Williams could win game eight, Gleason would have Kerr for the decisive contest. White Sox fans felt hopeful.

Had they seen Williams the eve of game eight, they might not have been so optimistic. According to Lefty's account, he received a phone call after finishing dinner and was told that if his team won the next day, he would be shot.

That may or may not have been true, but Williams, who had yet to see any money from the gamblers, took no chances. He pitched like a twenty-year-old rookie and was knocked out in the first inning. The Reds took a 4–0 lead in that stanza and never trailed in that game, eventually winning, 10–3.

Williams, who had won twenty-three games and tossed five shutouts during the regular season, became the first pitcher in Major League history to lose three World Series games. Cicotte, the best pitcher in the American League, had gone 1–2 with an ERA that was a full run higher than his regular-season ERA. Two aces had come up almost empty. It was suspect, to say the least.

Comiskey wasn't eager for any kind of investigation. The sad truth was, gambling had permeated baseball during that era, and few teams were exempt. Comiskey may have doubted that his ballplayers would have been foolish enough to throw the Series, but he wasn't so sure that some of them might not have been booting games.

In the end, the gamblers didn't come through anyway, stiffing the players for much of the promised sum. Jackson testified to a Chicago grand jury that he actually tried to give the money back, emphatic that he had played to win the Series.

The rumors dragged on through the 1920 season, but the roster was still strong. For the first time in Major League history, Chicago featured four twenty-game winners: Faber (23–13), Williams (22–14), Cicotte (21–10), and Kerr (21–9). Only the 1971 Baltimore Orioles have matched that feat.

The White Sox, Indians, and Yankees were enmeshed in a tight pennant race when, late in the season, Cicotte confessed to taking money. He and the other seven were indicted on September 28, 1920. With a heavy heart, Comiskey suspended them, pending the outcome of the trial.

In the short run, that meant that Chicago's pennant chances were dead. The Sox finished second, two games out.

The long-term implications were far more dramatic. After a long trial, the players were acquitted, but Comiskey didn't let them back on the team; he couldn't. A commissioner, Kenesaw Landis, had been appointed that year to run the league in response to a variety of baseball ills. Never before had there been one man who could make such a large impact on the game. Landis ignored the court case and banned the players for life. This move forever established the power of baseball's commissioner and changed the way the game was run and organized.

As for the players involved, none ever played an organized game again. They became forever known as the Black Sox: eight men who threw away their careers for a little money. The scandal destroyed the potential Hall of Fame career of Joe Jackson. Shoeless Joe still has the third-best career batting average of all time, .356, behind Ty Cobb and Rogers Hornsby.

Players swore that when he hit the ball, it made a different, harsher sound. Babe Ruth himself admitted that he copied Jackson's swing. Now Jackson was out of the game for good.

Jackson apologists, who insist he played to win, forget that he kept the $5,000 he was given by gamblers and also that he signed an affidavit confession his role in the fix. His abilities certainly merit induction into the Hall of Fame, yet for many, his character is the issue.

Regardless of Jackson, the 1920s were rough for Sox fans. With such a large portion of the team suspended, the White Sox never finished higher than fifth place the rest of the decade. The competitive balance of the league had been upended. There was now no team to challenge the New York Yankees in the American League, and the Yanks, with pitcher-turned-hitter Babe Ruth swinging for the fences, dominated baseball.

In Chicago, bright spots were few and far between.

A Dark Era: The 1920s

In the spring of 1923, the White Sox trained in Texas, near Baylor University. The team scrimmaged with the local college and their ace, Ted Lyons. Lyons was cuffed around a bit, but his control and toughness impressed Comiskey. He would eventually offer Lyons a $1,000 signing bonus to play for the Sox after graduation.

Lyons joined the team that July and ended up 2–1 on the season. By 1925, Lyons led the majors with twenty-one wins. He played for Chicago for twenty-one years, the longest term of service in team history, and was elected to the Hall of Fame in 1955.

By 1927, Sox manager Ray Schalk was rebuilding the team. Lyons was the anchor, and the pitching staff was solid with Tommy Thomas and Ted Blankenship. The infield was led by third baseman Willie Kamm and the outfield by Bibb Falk. For a few months, the Sox challenged the Yankees for first place, but then New York turned on the jets; with Ruth socking sixty homers, the Yanks ran away with the pennant.

It wasn't a bad year, but everything needs to be put in context: that was one of the best finishes by a Sox team in the 1920s. And on October 16, 1931, Charles Comiskey died of heart failure, having never recovered from the Black Sox scandal.

Looking back, Comiskey has to share some of the blame. A pitiless negotiator and notorious tightwad, his players grew to hate him. Clearly, not all of the "Chicago Eight" were fully involved in the scandal, but just as clearly, they all resented Comiskey.

Family Matters: The 1930s and 1940s

Upon Comiskey's death, his son J. Louis Comiskey took over day-to-day operations of the White Sox. Like any good son, Lou wanted to improve upon what his father had built. For a while, he did, acquiring key players like shortstop Luke Appling. The team finished third in 1936 and 1937. This record might seem relatively modest, but was considered an improvement among fans. Appling's .388 won him the 1936 batting title (the first of two), an average that remains the franchise record.

Perhaps the most important event in White Sox history that decade was the creation of the All-Star Game. Comiskey Park hosted the first one in 1933, and Yankee Babe Ruth was nice enough to smack a home run that game, helping give the American League their 4–2 victory. Thanks for the memories, Babe.

The Sox, at times, seemed snakebitten. Promising pitcher Monty Stratton, who had gone 15–5 in 1937 and 15–9 in 1938, accidentally shot himself during the off-season. The bullet pierced the femoral artery in Stratton's leg, and he never pitched for the White Sox again.

Meanwhile, Lou Comiskey was MIA. He had begun his ownership of the Sox by making trades and spending money to improve the team, but then he had become a near-recluse at the family's Eagle River, Wisconsin, getaway. Comiskey was often ill, a condition exacerbated by his alarming weight gain over the years.

Although Comiskey was well respected by his employees and players, the club began to drift again. Lou died in July of 1939, having never fully recovered from a bout of scarlet fever, and his death set off several months of legal wrangling over who really owned the club.

The public battle put the club's finances on the front page of the newspapers. The First National Bank of Chicago, which was trying to sell the club, announced that the White Sox had lost $675,029 from

1928 to 1939. A probate judge, however, upheld the family's claim that the team was on the road to solvency, and the White Sox remained a Comiskey property. Grace Comiskey, Lou's widow, took over the day-to-day operations of the club.

With the onset of World War II, the fortunes of the White Sox did not improve significantly. By 1944, the team was under the .500 mark and went through a series of managers, none of whom could get the job done. The Sox were no longer competitive, and in 1948 they lost 101 games.

By 1950, the Chicago White Sox were one of the worst franchises in baseball. They had not been to a World Series since 1919 and had not won one since 1917. From 1919 to 1950, the team finished second only once. The Sox finished fifteen or more games out of first place an unenviable twenty-eight of those thirty-two years and finished under the .500 mark twenty-one of those thirty-two seasons.

The Go-Go Sox: The 1950s

The Comiskeys decided to make a move. Grace Comiskey hired Frank "Trader" Lane as general manager after the dreadful 1948 season. Lane, the former president of the American Association, a Midwestern minor league, got to work.

He picked up young pitcher Billy Pierce from Detroit, and the next year he snagged second baseman and future Hall of Famer Nellie Fox. In April of 1951, he swung a three-cornered deal with the Indians and A's to get outfielder Orestes "Minnie" Minoso, the first black player in franchise history. In November of 1951, Lane traded for St. Louis Browns catcher Sherm Lollar. In 1954, he would sign shortstop Luis Aparicio out of Venezuela; after two years in the minors, the rookie debuted in 1956.

Lane's changes were making an impact. From 1952 to 1956 the Sox finished third, always behind the Yankees and the Cleveland Indians. But the team was competitive, with Pierce and veteran Virgil Trucks on the mound, and Fox, Lollar, Minoso, and shortstop Chico Carrasquel anchoring the defense. The team the press now called the "Go-Go Sox" for their aggressive baserunning was moving up.

In 1957, the White Sox hired Al Lopez to manage the team. Lopez, a former catcher, had previously managed the Cleveland Indians to their 1954 pennant win. He was considered a canny, tough skipper who might be able to get the Sox over the top.

After a pair of exciting second-place finishes, Lopez got the job done in 1959. As usual, the Go-Go Sox were not great hitters, with the exception of Nellie Fox. The pitching staff, though, had the best team-ERA in the league, 3.29, and the Sox had the best fielding average, .979. The Sox also led the majors in stolen bases with 113, twenty-nine more than the runner-up Los Angeles Dodgers.

When Grace Comiskey died in 1956, her son Chuck and daughter Dorothy vied for control of the team. After several contentious years, and just prior to the 1959 season, the Sox changed owners when the Comiskeys sold the club to a consortium of businessmen headed by Bill Veeck Jr., former owner of the Cleveland Indians. Chuck Comiskey retained a 46 percent interest in the team.

Veeck's father, Bill Veeck Sr., had been the president of the Cubs for many years. The younger Veeck had been employed by the club as treasurer at the tender age of nineteen. Eight years later, the younger Veeck quit the Cubs organization to strike out on his own. In 1941, the twenty-seven-year-old Veeck purchased a sagging minor-league franchise in Milwaukee. Four years later he sold the club for $275,000.

Veeck was a master promoter. During his tenure with the St. Louis Browns in the late 1940s and early 1950s, he was the man who brought three-foot, seven-inch Eddie Gaedel to pinch-hit in a game against the Tigers. Veeck's trademark was offering prizes, hosting promotions, and generally ensuring that the fans had a good time at the ballpark.

1959: The Sox Are in the Series!

Veeck's promotional savvy, combined with the Sox' performance on the field, generated an all-time White Sox Chicago attendance record in 1959 of 1,443,144. With an MVP year for Fox, twenty-two victories for Early Wynn (which earned him the Cy Young Award), and the league lead in steals for Aparicio, the Sox won the American League championship with a 94–60 mark, five games better than the Indians.

The city of Chicago, which had last seen a World Series contest with the Cubs in 1945, went crazy over the Sox. The crush for tickets was immense, and a sellout crowd greeted the Sox and their National League opponents, the Los Angeles Dodgers, for game one of the World Series on October 1.

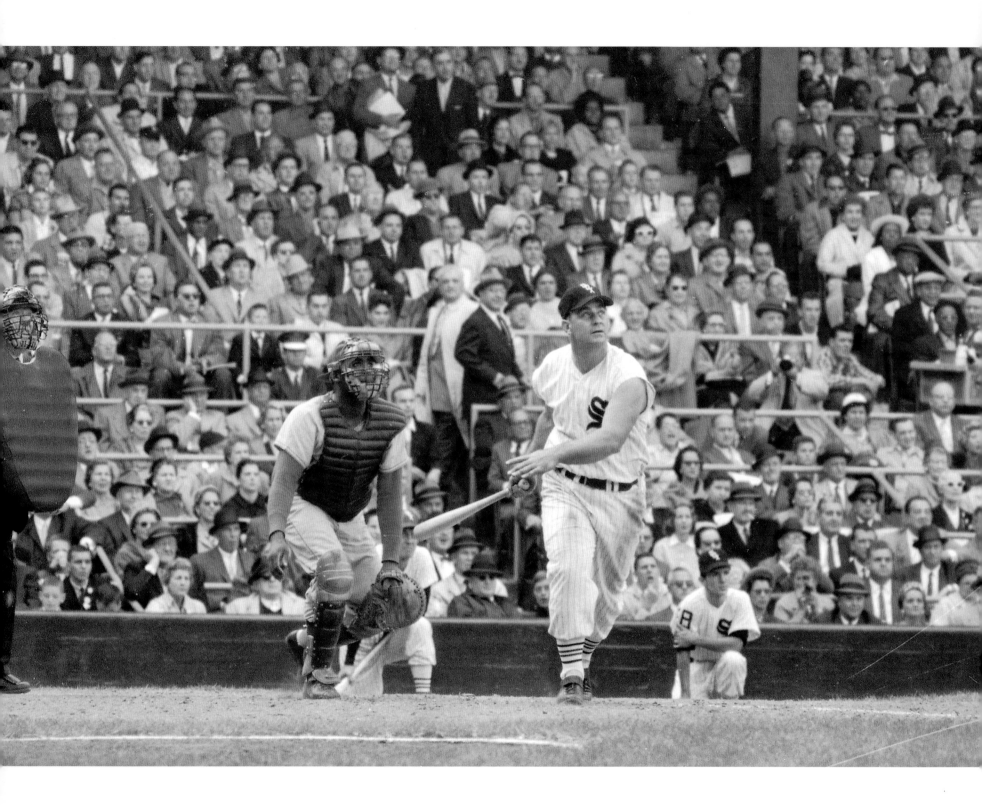

The Sox wasted little time in the contest, scoring a pair of runs in the bottom of the first inning and then erupting for seven runs in the third. First baseman Ted Kluszewski belted a two-run shot in that stanza, then crushed a second two-run homer in the next inning. Leading 11–0, Wynn cruised to victory.

But the Dodgers evened the series the next day behind pitchers Johnny Podres and Larry Sherry, who combined to scatter eight hits in a 4–3 Dodger win.

The scene switched to Los Angeles, and Dodger pitching proved to be the key factor in the next game. Big Don Drysdale gave up eleven hits but only one run in a 3–1 Dodger win in game three. The next day, L.A. veteran Gil Hodges drilled a home run in the eighth to snap a 4–4 tie and give the home team a 5–4 win and a 3–1 series advantage.

Game five was a gem, as the Sox' Bobby Shaw, Billy Pierce, and Dick Donovan outpitched Sandy Koufax and Stan Williams to win a 1–0 nail-biter. These three became the first trio of pitchers to throw a shutout in World Series history. The lone run came in the fourth, when Fox singled, went to third on a Jim Landis single, and scored when Lollar hit into a double play.

Back in Chicago, Wynn started game six but didn't have enough. The Dodgers scored two runs in the third and six in the fourth to spark a 9–3 rout. Disgruntled Sox fans filed out of Comiskey Park early. They should have stayed; it would be the last World Series appearance for the Sox in the twentieth century.

Selling the Sox: The 1960s

There was optimism in Chicago in 1960, and the fans turned out in record numbers again: 1.6 million, another franchise record. They came to see the White Sox and Veeck's newest innovation: the exploding scoreboard. Veeck installed small cannons behind the scoreboard that were fired whenever a Sox player hit a home run.

The promotion king was in poor health, and in 1961 Veeck sold the team to Arthur Allyn Jr.; the Sox became a subsidiary of Allyn's Artnell conglomerate. Chuck Comiskey sold his 46 percent and, for the first time in franchise history, a Comiskey was not involved with the club.

The 1960s were particularly agonizing for Sox fans. In 1963, the team won ninety-four games but never really challenged the Yankees, who won 104. In 1964, the team won ninety-eight games, but the Yankees once again did better, winning ninety-nine. (The musical *Damn Yankees* might have hit Broadway a decade before, but in the mid-1960s its underdog sentiment hit a nerve with Chicagoans.)

Juan Pizzaro had his best season as a major leaguer in 1964, going 19–9 with 163 strikeouts and a place on the All-Star team. Peters, whom many sportswriters thought was something of a fluke, came back in 1964 to win a league-high 20 games.

Try as they might, the Sox couldn't beat the Yankees in 1964, dropping their first ten games to the New Yorkers before defeating them on August 11. The Sox chased New York throughout the latter part of that summer but never caught them. Damn Yankees.

Eddie Stanky, a former player who had managed the Browns in the mid-1950s, took over the managerial reins from Al Lopez in 1966 and guided the club to fourth-place finishes in 1966 and 1967. The latter was an exciting season, as the White Sox battled the Minnesota Twins, Boston Red Sox, and Detroit Tigers for the American League pennant. No Sox regular hit better than .241 that season, yet Chicago stayed in the hunt until the last week of the season.

In 1968, major turnover transpired once more: Stanky, who had run-ins with the media when he was managing in St. Louis, accused the Chicago press of negativism and refused to talk to them. He also banned his players from doing so, and to make sure they complied, he ordered his coaches to dress in the players' locker room to stand guard.

That was too much for the White Sox brass, who hired Lopez midseason and fired Stanky. Ironically, they told the media before they told Stanky.

Meanwhile, Allyn was looking to sell; despite a fantastic pennant race in 1967, the team had drawn under one million fans for the third consecutive year.

In 1969, Allyn sold the Sox to his younger brother John. It didn't make any difference, as the Sox finished fifth in 1969 and last in 1970, losing 106 games.

Short Shorts and Disco Demolition: The 1970s

Though most of us would like to glide on past the 1970s as if they'd never happened, the decade saw improvement in some areas for the

Sox. They started by hiring Chuck Tanner to manage the team. And from 1972 to 1973, Chicago was in first place for at least part of the season; unfortunately, that was never in September, when it counted.

Bill Melton, a slugging third baseman led the league in homers in 1971 with thirty-three. The Sox also acquired the extremely talented but enigmatic Dick Allen. With his lightning swing, Allen came within a few hits of the Triple Crown in 1972. With a league-leading thirty-seven home runs and 113 RBI, Allen hit .308 to come in third behind the Twins' Rod Carew at .318 and the Royals' Lou Piniella at .312. Allen also led the league in slugging percentage (.603) and walks (99) and was second in total bases (305). Allen easily won the MVP. In 1974, Allen again led the league in homers with thirty-four.

Ironically for a club with a history of strong pitching, the Sox bullpen was not up to par. Tanner was constantly battling the front office to sign better players, and in 1975, John Allyn sold the club back to Bill Veeck.

Veeck, whose health by this time had improved, once again had the Sox leading the league in promotions. Two of those promotions remain among the most talked about in baseball history. In 1976, at the urging of his wife, Veeck outfitted his team in shorts. That's right, 100 years of baseball tradition be damned . . . this club is going out there looking like a softball team. The Chi-Sox wore the black shorts exactly once, in the first game of a doubleheader on August 8. In the second game, the shorts were in the dustbin of history and the Sox were back in their pants. Said Mrs. Veeck: "They were not totally a gag thing. It got very hot in Comiskey Park."

Another event that decade put Chicago on the baseball map, but not for reasons they wanted. Bill's son Mike had some control of the marketing then and he dreamed up, in conjunction with a local DJ, a stunt that would live in infamy. This was in 1979, the heyday of disco music. For a doubleheader one evening, fans were invited to bring their disco records to the park. The idea was that between games of the

doubleheader, fans would bring their records to the field, where they would be burned. It was billed as "Disco Demolition Night." It would be the first and last such event.

It was an unmitigated disaster. As soon as DJ Steve Dahl blew up a small crate of records, an inebriated, insane crowd flooded the field, tore apart the grass, torched more records, and set numerous bonfires. It was mayhem, complete and total chaos. Needless to say, the second game of the twin bill was forfeited to the visiting and stunned Tigers (and they'd thought Detroit was wild!).

That was the story of the White Sox in those days: black shorts and exploding disco records.

Strangely enough, the promotions, combined with some solid playing, did some good. In 1977, the Sox, led by speedy Ralph Garr and powerful Richie Zisk, finished second. Another franchise record was set, with 1.66 million in attendance.

Even so, Veeck was hanging on by his fingernails. The era of free agency had begun, and the Sox couldn't really compete. From 1978 to 1980, the team finished twenty, fourteen, and twenty-six games out.

Home Improvement: The 1980s and 1990s

Veeck sold the team in 1980 to local businessmen Jerry Reinsdorf and Eddie Einhorn. Reinsdorf and Einhorn, unlike Veeck, had deep pockets. They scored a huge coup by prying free agent Carlton Fisk away from the Red Sox in 1981. The Sox also picked up the hulking Greg Luzinski that year. In 1983, the Sox had two twenty-game winners in La Marr Hoyt (24–10) and Rich Dotson (22–7), as well as Rookie of the Year Ron Kittle, who was third in the league in home runs with thirty-five. Chicago, with manager Tony LaRussa pulling the strings, went 99–63 to win the division by an astounding twenty games.

LaRussa's last job had been as the skipper of the minor league Iowa Oaks. But he was tough, fair, and a fanatic about preparation.

LaRussa was among the first of a new generation of managers who studied opposing teams' tendencies and tried to take advantage of potential weaknesses. Under his care, the Sox dominated the regular season, and many fans expected a World Series appearance.

That was the good news. The bad news was that after the Sox won game one, 2–1, behind Hoyt, the Orioles dominated the American League Championship Series over the next three games. The Sox managed only one run in twenty-eight innings, losing the series in four games.

For the rest of the 1980s, the White Sox topped the .500 mark only once with an 85–77 record that was good for third place in the Western Division in 1985. LaRussa was gone by 1986, soon to be followed by solid rookie Bobby Bonilla, traded to the Pirates.

Reinsdorf and Einhorn soon realized they were losing the battle for Chicagoans' hearts (and dollars) to the crosstown Cubs. Their solution was to build a new ballpark—at the expense of the City of Chicago. The two men announced that the team would be moving to St. Petersburg, Florida, if a new stadium was not built. After an extended wrangle, Governor Jim Thompson realized that he didn't want to be known as the man who let the White Sox get away. He pushed through legislation to fund the "New Comiskey Park," which was built in 1991.

From 1984 to 1989, the team never finished better than third, turning in three consecutive fifth-place finishes from 1986 to 1988. In 1990, they achieved a second-place finish, with ace reliever Bobby Thigpen setting a Major League record with fifty-seven saves.

The new Comiskey Park went up across the street from the old one, and by 1993, the White Sox were back as contenders. Slugger Frank Thomas, who came up in 1990, began putting up serious numbers, socking a franchise-record forty-one homers in 1993 and adding a .317 batting average and 128 RBI. Pitcher Jack McDowell, with a 22–10 record, won the Cy Young Award.

But the Sox lost the American League Championship Series to the Toronto Blue Jays in 1993. In 1994, Thomas continued to put up Triple Crown numbers with thirty-eight home runs, a .353 batting average, and 101 RBI, all of which were close to the league leaders. The Sox were in first with a 67–46 record (ahead of the previous year's winning percentage) when the Major League Baseball season ended with a players' strike on August 12.

Both leagues split from two to three divisions in 1994, and from 1995 to 1999, the White Sox finished behind the Cleveland Indians, who appeared in two World Series during that time. With Thomas ripping forty-three dingers to go with a .328 batting average, the White Sox finally broke through with another title in 2000. But the result remained the same—a first-round loss, this time to the Seattle Mariners.

Still, the Sox were often in contention over the next few seasons. Outfielder Magglio Ordonez was brought up in 1997, and by 1999 he was a perennial All-Star.

In 1998, the Sox drafted outfielder Aaron Rowand and lefty pitcher Mark Buehrle. They also acquired righty Jon Garland from the Cubs and first baseman Paul Konerko from the Reds. Those four players would be the cornerstones of the franchise for the next several years. Buehrle was what scouts described as an "inning eater," meaning he was durable and pitched deep into almost every game he started. In 2004, he led the American League by pitching 245⅓ innings. Garland was not as durable, but his intimidating size (6'6") and blazing fastball generated at least ten wins annually. Rounding out the stars, Rowand

proved to be a defensive leader for the Sox, while Konerko emerged as one of the better clutch players in the league.

A Team for the New Century

In 2000, the White Sox hired general manager Kenny Williams. With the aforementioned four ballplayers as the core of the squad, Williams set to work on his team. In 2002, he acquired infielder Willie Harris and another left-hander, Damaso Marte. And more importantly, he hired former Sox All-Star shortstop Ozzie Guillen to manage the team.

Guillen, at forty, was one of the youngest managers in the majors. But with Williams's help, he remade the White Sox in his own image: a hustling, smart team capable of manufacturing runs as well as slugging it out with competitors. Williams bristled at the notion that his club was a "small-ball" squad.

"We win all sorts of ways," he told the Associated Press. "We can slug it with the best of them, but sometimes, we have to scratch [runs] out."

On January 31, 2003, the White Sox signed a twenty-three-year deal with U.S. Cellular for $68 million to rename their ballpark U.S. Cellular

Field. A financial windfall for Sox ownership no doubt, but White Sox fans quickly nicknamed the new field "the Cell."

The White-Hot White Sox

At the beginning of the 2005 season, the Sox took off, and by the All-Star break they owned the best record in the majors. They went on to win their division by six games.

Williams had acquired a number of players prior to the 2005 season, including righty Dustin Hermanson, outfielders Jermaine Dye and Scott Podsednik, and veteran hurler Orlando "El Duque" Hernandez. In past years, when the Sox would traditionally melt in the August heat of a pennant race, the team's depth carried them through.

The postseason was where the White Sox often struggled, and even their own fans were initially apprehensive as Chicago began the divisional playoffs against the defending World Champion Boston Red Sox.

They needn't have worried. Chicago pounded their Boston foes in game one, winning 14–2. The next two games were closer, but second baseman Tadahito Iguchi, acquired prior to the season from Japan, blasted a three-run homer to help win game two, 5–4. El Duque turned in three huge relief innings to hold off the Sox in game three, 5–3. With the sweep, Chicago had won its first postseason series since 1917.

The Los Angeles Angels of Anaheim were next in the American League Championship Series. After playing poorly in the opener, a 3–2 Angels win, Chicago got consecutive complete games from Buehrle, Garland, Freddy Garcia, and Jose Contreras to defeat the Angels.

There was a controversial play in game two that Angels fans will doubtless point to as the turning point of the series. That occurred when Angels catcher Josh Paul failed to tag the Sox' A. J. Pierzynski in the bottom of the ninth after Pierzynski had swung and missed at strike three. The game was tied 1–1. Pierzynski thought Paul had muffed the ball, and took off for first. Umpire Doug Eddings ruled that Paul had not caught the ball (television replays showed that he did), and Pierzynski was safe. Moments later, an RBI double by Joe Crede won the game.

While Pierzynski's play was a key one, the way the White Sox staff pitched in that series, it's hard to imagine the Angels could have strung together enough hits to score more than a handful of runs. Big plays happen in seven-game series, not five-game blowouts.

So this was it: the Sox were in their first World Series since 1959, trying to erase an eighty-seven-year-long string of failure. In the Series, Chicago faced the Houston Astros, who were playing in their first-ever World Series. It was promoted as a pitchers' duel, as both teams boasted outstanding starting pitching and deep bull pens. The pitchers didn't exactly dominate on either side, but both teams provided tons of drama.

The first game was a 5–3 nail-biter, with Sox closer Bobby Jenks leading a Chicago bullpen that shut down the Astros with men in scoring position in the eighth. In game two, the Sox fell behind 4–0 but roared back thanks to a grand slam by Paul Konerko. But Houston tied the game, and then came a play that must have made old Shoeless Joe smile. In the bottom of the ninth, in a little place that, well, no matter what the sign says, will always really be Comiskey Park, a miracle happened. A walk-off homer by Scott Podsednik, who had hit a total of zero home runs in the 2005 regular season, set off a party in the South Side that just continued and continued for the next three days. It was an instant Series classic, and he joined a long line of spot players who rise to the occasion in the glare of the Fall Classic.

Games three and four were in Houston, and each also provided new classic moments. Houston tied game three in the eighth at 5–5 after Chicago had overcome an earlier four-run deficit with five in the fifth. And then a long slog began: For five more innings and about two more hours, Chicago pitchers let Astros on base and then shut them down without allowing a run. The White Sox bats, meanwhile, were quiet until Geoff Blum came up in the top of the fourteenth and matched the feat of his teammate Podsednik. He pulled a homer into the right-field bleachers to give the White Sox the lead. They added an insurance run, held off the Astros in the bottom of the fourteenth, and a World Series–record five hours and forty-one minutes after it had started, Chicago had won game three and was one win away from making history.

Game four was another close one, as close as one can make it. Houston starter Brandon Backe bravely held the Sox scoreless through seven, while Chicago's Freddy Garcia did the same to the Astros. In the eighth, Houston went to its relief ace, Brad Lidge, who was still smarting from having given up Podsednik's homer. Chicago scratched out a single run against Lidge, setting the stage for the ninth inning.

Jenks was on again and he got big help from shortstop Juan Uribe. For

the second out, Uribe dove into the stands behind third to snag a foul pop. Then to make the White Sox champs, he made a great charge on a soft grounder and fired to first to light the fuse on a South Side celebration.

"I've been here for seven years," Konerko told ESPN.com's Jayson Stark, "and on this team, I've been here the longest, along with Frank (Thomas). But compared with all the fans and all the people who put up with the frustrations of this team for all those years, that's nothing. Those are the people who have suffered for a long, long time. But when you win, people don't forget you. So now, we'll always be remembered as part of the team that finally jumped over that wall."

It was a wall that was eighty-eight years tall, a wall built by bad luck, bad moves, and bad personnel. But it came crashing down with the scrappy White Sox. And how good were the Sox in 2005? In the history of the Major Leagues, three teams have swept the World Series in the same year that they were in first place for the entire season: the 1927 New York Yankees (yes, those Yankees of Ruth and Gehrig), the 1990 Cincinnati Reds, and the 2005 Chicago White Sox.

And they did it without wearing black shorts or blowing up one vinyl record. ★

Members of Chicago's Roseland North meet with
West Tokyo players, the first Japanese team in a
Little League World Series, 1967.

Little League ★★★

Only fifty guys get to play pro baseball in Chicago . . . but they only play on two fields. That leaves the rest of the diamonds in the city open to be filled with kids. Which is as it should be; this is a kids' game, after all. And Chicago has a youth baseball tradition half as long but just as deep as its big-league equivalent.

Whether they played in Boise, Baton Rouge, or Brooklyn, pretty much every Major Leaguer worth his sunflower seeds came up through the ranks of Little League baseball. White Sox owner Bill Veeck was impressed by a twelve-year-old Little Leaguer in Easton, Maryland, named Harold Baines and eventually made Baines his first-round draft pick when the player came of age in 1977. Some Major League players even came up through Chicago's own sandlots, including pitcher Bill Gullickson and outfielder Bobby Mitchell.

Little League baseball was born in 1939 in Williamsport, Pennsylvania, when a twenty-nine-year-old sandpaper plant worker named Carl Stotz came up with the idea of a league for youngsters aged nine to twelve. What better way to introduce kids to sportsmanship and teamwork?

Stotz and two other coaches organized a league that summer and, in what was considered a unique idea at the time, solicited local businesses and individuals as sponsors. As good ideas do, this one quickly caught on, and soon there were competitive leagues in town. But the ideals of sportsmanship carried through, and the raiding of players from the competition was not allowed by anyone.

Following World War II, Little Leagues began to spring up in small towns throughout Pennsylvania and New Jersey. By the first Little League World Series (then known as the National Little League Tournament) in 1947, there were sixty teams in fifteen leagues in the two states. Williamsport's own Maynard Midgets won the first championship that year. In addition, the first Little League graduate entered into the ranks of professional play in 1947, with former Little Leaguer Allen "Sonny" Yearick of the 1939 Lycoming Dairy team signing with the Boston Braves.

Only ten years after its inception, Stotz's Little League had expanded to 307 leagues in the United States. A feature in the popular *Saturday Evening Post* that year exposed millions of readers to the history of league, and newsreels showing highlights from the 1948 Little League World Series were seen by millions of Americans. The media exposure worked its magic, and Stotz was deluged with requests from communities around the country—and the world—about starting local leagues.

Enter the Boys of Chicago

Chicago earned its place at the table in 1956. Not only did the city officially launch a league that year, but it also hosted the first nationwide Little League Congress to elect district representatives and to better coordinate the Little League World Series. And the following season saw the first non-American team win the LLWS; Mexican pitcher Angel Macias threw the first perfect game in a championship final.

In 1967, Chicago boys finally made it to the big stage: Howard J. Lamade Stadium in Williamsport, in central Pennsylvania. The kids from the Roseland North league made it all the way to the finals before falling to a team from Japan. Regardless of the loss in the championship game, Roseland North's showing in Williamsport meant that Chicago was home to the best Little League team in America.

The 1968 season saw another Chicago team, the Westlawn Little League, defeat Marion 9–2 for the Illinois championship, led by pitcher John Kappel, who fired a one-hitter in the championship game.

Westlawn returned to the championship game in 1972, edging West Frankfort 2–0 in the state semifinals and then stopping Bradley-Bourbonnais 5–0 in nine innings. In the championship game that year, the contest was tied 0–0 after eight innings. But a bases-loaded walk scored the first run, and Westlawn's Mike Powers lashed a grand slam to put the game away despite suffering a pulled leg muscle earlier in the game.

The Jackie Robinson West Little League

The 1980s saw the Jackie Robinson West Little League dominate the state tournament, with three championships in five years. The team first won it all in 1983, stopping Bradley-Bourbonnais 9–4, which included two-run home runs by Barry Freeman and Bryan Street in the fifth inning.

Jackie Robinson West then became the second Chicago-based Little League team to win a Northeast Regional championship, beating Wabash, Indiana, 7–1. Jackie Robinson West had a relatively easy tournament, whipping Taylor Northwest Little League, the Michigan champs, 4–0 in the first round and dominating Sioux City, Iowa, 8–1 to reach the final.

In the Little League World Series, Jackie Robinson West was matched up against the eventual champions from Marietta, Georgia. The South

Regional champs piled up seven runs in the first inning to coast to a 7–2 win. Jackie Robinson West finished third in the tournament, beating the Arabian Gulf team from Saudi Arabia, 15–0, and the Sacramento, California team, the Western champions, 5–0. Interestingly, the Saudi team, which was made up primarily of American boys whose parents were working in the region, was the first team from the Middle East to play in the tournament.

The following year Jackie Robinson West claimed the regional championship again, becoming the first Little League to win consecutive crowns. Norrice Quarrels, a veteran of the 1983 squad, led the team to three consecutive shutouts in the sectional tourney, 15–0 over Libertyville, and then 4–0 and 5–0 over Joliet Belmont. Quarrels struck out eleven batters and added a home run in the title game.

In 1987, the Chicago team was stunned, 2–1, by the Elgin Classic Little League and was forced to play through the losers' bracket to get back to the finals. Jackie Robinson West then defeated Chicago Westlawn, 10–5, Galesburg National, 6–5, and Paris, 9–6, to reach the final round.

Jackie Robinson West had to win two games to capture the title, as the series was a double-elimination tournament. In the first game, Chicago pitcher Charles McGraw threw a complete-game 4–2 win. In the second game, McGraw hit two home runs to lead a crushing attack as Jackie Robinson West took an easy 16–3 victory. Pelly Mott was the winning pitcher.

The 1990s saw Westlawn Little League return to the winner's circle, whipping Norridge, 3–1. Kevin Goshorn struck out sixteen batters and allowed only four hits in the win. This was Westlawn's third state title, tying them with Jackie Robinson West for the most state titles by a city Little League team.

But the next season, Westlawn broke that tie, coming out of the losers' bracket to beat Bradley-Bourbonnais American Little League, 12–7 and 10–3, for their fourth state title.

The team returned no players from the 1999 champions. First baseman Alex Robles was 4-for-4 with 6 RBI in the first game. In the second contest, eight different Westlawn players contributed hits, and they scored in every inning but the sixth.

With the win, Westlawn joined the Kankakee Jaycees Little League as the only four-time state titlists in Illinois history. Since Roseland's premiere in the LLWS, a total of seven Chicago-based teams have won the Illinois State Little League championship, but only one, Jackie Robinson West Little League, won the Regional Tournament, in 1983.

In 1999 Burkina Faso, a small, landlocked republic in Africa, became the one hundredth country with a Little League program. Carl Stotz's dream of more than sixty years ago has become a global one with youngsters the world over introduced to the great game of baseball and the camaraderie of team sports.

The success and excitement generated over Little League in general, and in the Chicago area in particular, illustrate that it isn't only the professional teams that garner fan enthusiasm and bring people out to the ballpark time and again. The Chicago-area Little League teams have been instrumental, particularly in the past two decades, in providing the city's young boys and girls with a positive recreational outlet and instilling in them a love of the game. ★

The Chicago Whales ★ ★ ★

For more than forty years, until the eve of World War I, the Cubs and White Sox, in their various guises and nicknames, were the only game in town. Likewise in most major cities that boasted big-league teams. There were occasional challengers to the hegemony that was "organized baseball," as the two major leagues were rather pompously called, but most came quickly to nothing. One such league, however, had an impact on Chicago baseball, then and now.

Riding the Fast Track

In 1913, a group of businessmen from around the country opted to form a new minor league, the Columbia League, with aspirations toward eventual major league status. The league had a distinct Windy City flair, as Chicago entrepreneur John T. Powers was behind its formation and served as its president. Powers wanted to build the new league slowly, an unpopular stance; he was replaced after just a year by James Gilmore. The league, renamed the Federal League in 1914, was on the fast track.

In 1914, with Gilmore's blessing, they became a major league by raiding squads in both the American and National leagues for talent.

The Chicago franchise, initially known as the Chi-Feds, was not bashful about stealing players. They signed Cubs shortstop Joe Tinker to play and manage the squad in 1914. Tinker, in turn, signed Pittsburgh Pirates pitcher Claude Hendrix, who led the league in wins with twenty-nine, and Dutch Zwilling, who led the league in home runs with sixteen. Zwilling had been with the White Sox in 1910 and had toiled in the minors for three years before signing with the Whales.

The Whales ultimately lost the pennant to the Indianapolis Hoosiers by one-and-a-half games, but they won another important battle. They attracted more fans to their final-day showdown than either the Cubs or the White Sox, both teams also with home games that day. But it was a faint and short-lived victory at the turnstiles.

The Closest Pennant Race

The next season, the team, now renamed the Chicago Whales, went 86–66. They ended the season in a virtual tie for the Federal League pennant, finishing percentage points ahead of St. Louis.

The pennant race was *on* that year, coming down to a three-game competition between the St. Louis Terriers, the Pittsburgh Rebels, and the Whales. With all three teams within a game of each other the final week, Chicago finished at 86–66 and the Terriers at 87–67. (The Whales had lost two games to rainouts.) Meanwhile, despite a strong final week, Pittsburgh eventually finished 86–67.

The numbers may have been close, but there could only be one pennant winner. That honor was bestowed on the Whales on the basis of winning percentage: Chicago was at .566, St. Louis at .565, and Pittsburgh at .562. That 1915 Federal League pennant race represents the closest in baseball history, with the top three teams within .004 of each other.

Proud of his Whales, Tinker was in a competitive spirit and narrowed it on Chicago. He called for a three-way playoff between the Cubs, Sox, and the new Federal League champions to decide the city's best team. The other two Chicago teams declined Tinker's offer, so Whales fans took what was, to them, the next logical step: they declared their team "the Champions of Chicago."

Watching the Whales Work at Weeghman

The home of the Whales was the lofty Weeghman Park. Owner Charles Weeghman had commissioned architect Zachary Taylor Davis to create the country's greatest ballpark, and Davis had obliged. His creation contained 16,000 seats, including 2,000 ten-cent bleacher seats in the outfield. Every detail was addressed, to the extent that Kentucky bluegrass was planted in the infield and outfield. Davis's care clearly had a lasting impact: Weeghman Park would eventually come to be known as Wrigley Field.

The Whales were fairly successful at the gate in both 1914 and 1915. But the Federal League as a whole was struggling. Both the National League and the American League had filed lawsuits during the 1914 season to induce the Federal League owners to cease and desist raids on their teams. Meanwhile, the Federal League owners had filed an antitrust suit in federal court against what they

contended was a monopoly by organized baseball. Though the Federal League was foundering by this time, it had awakened big-league owners to potential trouble. In the authoritative *Total Baseball*, historian Harold Dellinger called the Federal League "as severe a threat to the status quo as any league in the history of baseball."

By 1915, the lawsuits had taken their toll on the new league's coffers. The Federal League owners were losing much more money than they bargained for and finally agreed to settle out of court. Just as it had grown quickly, the Federal League quickly dissolved. And yet, for the two years of its existence, the city of Chicago could proudly boast it was the seat of the ambitious league's flagship franchise.

Two big legacies of the Federal League remain a part of Chicago baseball history. The main suit filed by the Feds against organized baseball was heard by Judge Kenesaw Mountain Landis. This was the first time the ascetic disciplinarian came to the attention of baseball. Five years later, of course, he would be hired as the sport's first commissioner, and it was Landis who banned the eight members of the White Sox for allegedly throwing the 1919 World Series.

Also, when the Federal League disbanded, the National League knew a good park when they saw one, so they let Weeghman buy the Cubs. Guess where his new team got to play?

So, while it was little more than a long footnote in big-league history, Chicago fans can thank the Whales for Wrigley Field but blame the Feds for finding Landis. ★

*Charlie Grant, who played for the
Columbia Giants from 1899 to 1900, was
one of the great second basemen of his era.*

The Negro Leagues ★ ★ ★

From the latter part of the nineteenth century to the mid-twentieth, the Negro Leagues were the sole showcase for African American baseball players. Chicago evolved into one of the key cities in the history of the Negro Leagues, housing a number of memorable teams and featuring many outstanding ballplayers.

It should be noted that "Negro Leagues" is an umbrella term that describes the many baseball leagues and teams that featured African American ballplayers in the United States.

The Unions and the Columbia Giants

The Unions were the first organized African American team in the city. Formed in 1887 by manager Abe Jones, the Unions faced off against a number of semiprofessional teams in Chicago and throughout Illinois.

There is no record of the team's success that first year, but the club featured Bill Peters at first base, Grant Campbell at second base, Frank Scott at shortstop, Darby Cottman at third base, and Joe Campbell as the regular pitcher. The outfielders were Grant Campbell, Albert Hackley, and Frank Leland. In addition to his managerial chores, Jones was the regular catcher.

From 1891 until 1900, they were managed by first sacker Peters. Peters played first base until his retirement in 1894, the same year the Chicago Unions claimed the "Midwestern Colored Championship." Truth be told, there weren't a lot of other teams in the running, but the title probably sold a few tickets.

In 1899, shortstop Grant "Home Run" Johnson organized the Chicago Columbia Giants, a team that featured second baseman Charlie Grant; they were two of the earliest stars of the Negro Leagues.

Grant was a smooth-skinned, straight-haired black man, and in 1901, Baltimore Orioles manager John McGraw tried to pass him off as an American Indian named "Chief Tokahoma." It didn't work, and Grant ended up a Negro League star for many years.

Johnson, born in Findlay, Ohio, in 1874, was an anomaly in those light-hitting days: a shortstop who could belt home runs. He earned his nickname in 1894, belting sixty home runs in a 160-plus-game semipro season with the Findlay Sluggers.

He began his professional career in 1895 with the Page Fence Giants of Michigan. But when the Giants failed financially, Johnson took most of the players with him to Chicago in 1899. His Chicago Columbia

Opposite: *The Chicago American Giants, 1911. This team was considered one of the top Negro League teams in the West. Page 88: The 1919 Chicago American Giants. Rube Foster is fourth from the left in the top row. The team finished with a 17–9 record against other Negro League teams and won at least sixty games against outside competition. Page 89: Schorling's Park was the home of the Chicago American Giants in the 1920s.*

Giants quickly became known as a powerful, fundamentally sound unit.

In a September playoff series in 1899, the Columbia Giants swept the Unions, 4–2 and 6–2, with Johnson belting a home run in the latter contest. That same month, the Columbia Giants lost the "World's Colored Championship Series" to the Cuban X Giants of New York City, 7–4. Johnson struck another home run in that contest, and the slugger would eventually move on to play for a host of squads in the Negro Leagues.

Founding Father Rube Foster

In 1902, the most important figure in the history of the Negro Leagues made his way from his home state of Texas to join the Union Giants. His name was Andrew "Rube" Foster, and he became known as "the Father of the Negro Leagues."

Foster was a big kid: 6'2" and 200 pounds. In his early career, his fastball had three speeds: fast, faster, and lights out. He played that first year for forty dollars a month plus fifteen cents a day for meals.

He was known as Andrew until late in the summer of 1902, when he supposedly pitched and won an exhibition game against a team of white big-leaguers led by Philadelphia Athletics ace Rube Waddell. After his performance, he was forevermore known as "Rube" Foster.

Foster went a reported 30–1 that summer, and the Unions were the class Negro League team of the Midwest.

Foster knew his worth, however, and bounced around with various Negro League clubs for the next few years, including the Leland Giants in 1907. The Lelands, as they were called, were named for Frank Leland, who had broken away from the Chicago Union Giants in 1905. Foster was the ace of the Leland staff from 1907 to 1910.

Foster added a screwball to his array of fastballs, which made him even tougher to hit. Besides his amazing athletic ability, Foster also began to think about managing and organizing a team. The shaky financial situation of virtually every Negro League club at the turn of the twentieth century intrigued Foster, who might have made his living playing baseball but who also had a sharp eye for finances.

In 1911, Foster assembled a team of crack ballplayers called the Chicago American Giants and arranged for them to play their home games at the old Chicago White Sox Park at West Thirty-ninth Street and Wentworth Ave. Foster, by now a player-manager, began signing top

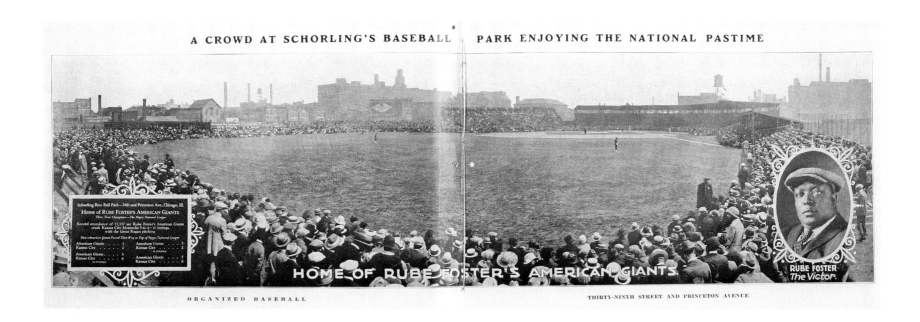

HOME OF RUBE FOSTER'S AMERICAN GIANTS.

RUBE FOSTER
The Victor.

ORGANIZED BASEBALL

THIRTY-NINTH STREET AND PRINCETON AVENUE

Negro League stars such as shortstop John Henry Lloyd, a future Hall of Famer, catcher Bruce Petway, and second baseman Bill Monroe.

Foster still took the mound, but with the acquisition of other hurlers such as Horace Jenkins and Frank Wickware, he pitched less and managed more. In 1911, the Giants had the best record of the Negro League teams in the West and claimed the unofficial "pennant." From that year until 1922, the Chicago American Giants were recognized as champions eleven of twelve years.

In addition to having great players (Chicago would also sign Negro League superstars Cristobal Torriente for the outfield and pitcher "Cannonball" Dick Redding), Foster's managerial style was to play aggressively at all times. His teams bunted, stole, and always looked to take the extra base. The sacrifice bunt was a Rube Foster staple.

Foster's club was the best-run, most popular team in the Negro Leagues of that era and one of the greatest teams of any league in the history of baseball. Chicago became the flagship city of black baseball during the late 1910s through 1930.

Dawn of a New League

Foster was also instrumental in organizing the first official black baseball league, the Negro National League, in 1920. Foster called a meeting of the owners of seven other Negro League teams that year and proposed adopting a formal charter.

"We are the ship," he said. "All else the sea."

The plan was simple: the charter mandated that they maintain a high level of professionalism in the league that would attract fans and new players.

It worked beautifully. Team schedules were synchronized, and a league schedule drawn up. The common practice of star players switching teams in midseason was greatly reduced. With stable team rosters, the league could better market itself.

Foster leased the Thirty-ninth Street Grounds from his white business partner, John Schorling, Charles Comiskey's son-in-law, who was a prominent tavern owner and manager of several amateur and semipro sandlot teams in the Greater Chicago area. Foster renovated the Grounds, also called Schorling's Park, adding bleachers and concession stands.

Ball games at Schorling's 9,000-capacity facility were almost formal affairs for African Americans who attended the games. Suits and ties were commonplace for men. Women were also welcome, and they likewise wore their Sunday best.

The Giants drew well. Schorling's Park featured comfortable seats and affordable refreshments, and on most days, the home side was victorious. African American fans came from many parts of the Midwest to see the team. In fact, there were reportedly times when visiting teams could not find enough hotels with rooms to accommodate them (hotels that allowed blacks were scarce), as the fans often got there first.

Foster, at forty-one, was at the top of the Negro Leagues, but his stay was brief. The stress of maintaining a whole league was telling. He had a nervous breakdown in 1926 and was hospitalized in a mental institution for the rest of his life. Foster died in 1930. He was elected to the Hall of Fame in 1981.

All-Stars in Chicago

In 1933, Gus Greenlee, owner of the Pittsburgh Crawfords, decided to promote a Negro League All-Star Game a few months after hearing that Major League Baseball had one in the works.

Greenlee reached a deal with Charles Comiskey to rent out Comiskey Park for the game. Chicago, which had been a mainstay of the Negro Leagues, was the obvious choice.

The *Pittsburgh Courier* and the *Chicago Defender*, the two leading black newspapers in the country, sponsored a contest in which the fans would vote for the members of the two all-star teams.

Despite the light drizzle, the first game drew well, and a team made up of all-stars from the West beat the Eastern all-stars, 11–7. Big Bill Foster, Rube Foster's half-brother who was himself a future Hall of Fame pitcher, picked up the win.

So successful was the game that the Negro League All-Star Game—called the East-West Game—would be held at Comiskey Park from 1933 until its demise in 1958. The game would sometimes draw more than 50,000

spectators, and in nine of its first eighteen seasons, it outdrew the Major League All-Star Game.

The contest became a huge social event for African Americans all over the country. Special trains from New York and Philadelphia brought fans to Chicago for the game. While the Chicago American Giants had some good years, the Kansas City Monarchs, with pitcher Satchel Paige, ruled the roost in the late 1930s and 1940s.

With the ascension of Monarch shortstop Jackie Robinson to the Brooklyn Dodgers in 1947, the Negro Leagues began a slow demise. By the late 1950s, black ballplayers were on every major league team, and the Negro Leagues were disbanded in 1960.

Although Chicago was perhaps the key city in Negro League history because of the perennial East-West Game at Comiskey and the presence of the Chicago American Giants, there were not a lot of native Chicagoans on the rosters. But among the better-known Chicago players was Jimmie Lyons, who played from 1910 to 1925. Lyons was one of the fastest players in the history of a league full of fast players. He was a superb outfielder for many teams, including the Chicago American Giants, the Detroit Stars, and the Indianapolis ABCs.

Other Chicago-born stars included Pat Patterson, an all-star third baseman with the Philadelphia Stars, Pittsburgh Crawfords, and Homestead Grays from 1934 to 1949; Put Powell, a pitcher who played for several Chicago-based squads, including the Chicago American Giants from 1930 to 1943; and Ralph Wyatt, a smooth-fielding shortstop with the Chicago American Giants, Homestead Grays, and Cleveland Buckeyes from 1941 to 1946. ★

The All-American Girls Professional Baseball League ★ ★ ★

The All-American Girls Professional Baseball League, or AAGPBL, had a franchise in Chicago during just one of its eleven seasons. However, that team finished in last place. But a Chicago man began the league, its offices were in Chicago, and a number of Chicago women starred in the league. The All-American Girls Professional Baseball League would never have gotten off the ground had things not begun to percolate in the Windy City.

Wartime Efforts

By late 1942, a number of minor-league baseball teams disbanded because of World War II. Healthy men, eighteen and older, were being drafted. That included healthy baseball men. Chicago Cubs owner Philip K. Wrigley became nervous in the wake of rumors that Major League Baseball would suspend operations because of the war.

Those rumors never reached fruition, but Wrigley ordered Cubs general manager Ken Sells to come up with ideas for filling Major League stadiums if the war took away too many talented ballplayers and reduced attendance. Sells's best idea was a women's softball league to try to regain some of the lost revenue if the stadiums ever did close.

Wrigley liked the idea, and called together a consortium of businessmen to work out the details. In the spring of 1943, the All-American Girls Softball League was born. The "Softball" in the league's name was soon changed to "Baseball" as the league changed its rules and reduced the size of the ball.

The choice was not unexpected. Women's softball was big in the Midwest and a growing sport in many areas of the country. Wrigley let Sells and Cubs scout Jack Sheehan set the rules, which combined elements of softball and baseball in its first year. Their most important decision was to allow players to lead off bases and steal, immediately making the game faster and more exciting than softball.

Wrigley proposed that the women's teams inhabit Major League parks and be scheduled to play when the big-league teams were out of town. But his fellow owners didn't think much of the idea, so Wrigley and his management team selected four non–Major League cities that would be close to league headquarters in Chicago.

The cities were Racine and Kenosha, Wisconsin; Rockford, Illinois; and South Bend, Indiana. Wrigley agreed to pay half the teams' expenses, with the host cities meeting the other half.

Edythe P...

Made in Chicago

After an extended search, 280 players were invited to tryouts in Chicago. The tryout was one day long, and at the end of the day, sixty players made the cut. Each team would have fifteen players, a coach, and a chaperone. Wrigley believed that having a well-known coach or ex-player in charge would generate fan curiosity. Three coaches were ex–big leaguers: Josh Billings, Eddie Stumpf, and Bert Niehoff. The fourth was Johnny Gottselig, a Canadian hockey star with numerous connections to sports franchises throughout Canada, where women's softball had caught on in recent years. Gottselig wasn't a baseball man, but he knew how to stock teams. He was the coach of the Racine Belles, winners of the first league championship in 1943.

Three of the first four players to be signed by the league were Chicago natives Ann Harnett, Edythe Perlick, and Clara Schillace. Schillace signed with Racine and manned the outfield with fellow Chicagoan Eleanor Dapkus, who signed later that spring. Dapkus was one of the early stars of the league, scoring sixty-five runs that year, with twenty-one extra base hits, including ten home runs.

Other Chicagoans who were signed that first year included Leola Brody, Josephine D'Angelo, Joanna Hageman, Pauline Pirok, Irene Ruhnke, Geraldine Shafranis, Josephine Skokan, and Dorothy Wind.

The 1943 season drew 176,612 fans, and the teams were well-supported in their host cities. The league expanded to six teams in 1944, and attendance went up again. Wrigley, tired of trying to manage a Major League Baseball team and a women's league concurrently, sold the women's league to Chicago advertising executive Arthur Meyerhoff.

Meyerhoff took the ball and ran with it. He began promoting the league and the players much more aggressively, having players visit wounded soldiers in veterans' hospitals, play exhibition games to support the Red Cross, and line up at the beginning of each game along the first and third baseline, forming a V for victory.

By 1945, attendance spiked to 450,313. Meyerhoff began a Junior League to serve as a minor league for the big clubs. He began moving spring training to places more exotic than Chicago—a blatant but successful move to get reporters to come out to cover the teams. In 1947, spring training was in Havana, Cuba. In 1948, it was in Opa-Locka, Florida.

The 1948 season was the apex. The league's ten teams drew 910,000 fans. Overhand pitching was made legal that year, and the Rockford Peaches, with their superb pitching staff, led by fastball pitcher Lois Florreich, won the first of three consecutive championships. Prior to this, pitchers were not allowed to wind up and throw. They stood on the mound and tossed the ball.

A mainstay of the Rockford dynasty was Charlene Barnett of Chicago at second base. Barnett batted fifth and was one of the best defensive infielders in the circuit. She and shortstop Dorothy "Snookie" Doyle of Los Angeles were the best middle infield tandem in the league.

Chicago's Share: The Colleens

The 1948 season also saw the formation of the Chicago Colleens, the only year an entry from Chicago played in the league. The Colleens, with

infielder Dolly Niemiec, a Chicago girl, finished last in 1948. But rather than disband them, the league turned them and the Springfield, Illinois, Sallies into barnstorming teams. The two squads played exhibition games in the Midwest in an attempt to bolster fan interest.

But television was on the rise, and Major League games, with all their stars back from World War II, were beginning to draw again. Something had to give, and eventually it was the AAGPBL. The league held on until 1954, but by then there were only five teams left.

Of the roughly six hundred women recruited from the entire North American continent who played in the league, about forty were from Chicago. In fact, the Midwest was heavily represented in the league, which was only logical, as that was where the teams were based.

The two biggest Chicago-based stars in the league were Perlick and Dapkus. Both played eight years in the league, from 1943 to 1950. The two, along with Schillace, led Racine to its first league title. Perlick ended up sixth in the league in all-time RBI (392). Dapkus was tenth on the career list (316), and also pitched, with a career record of 53–34.

Other Chicago-area players with strong careers in the league included catcher Annie O'Dowd, who played from 1949 to 1951 with the Kalamazoo Lassies; Pirok, a veteran who spent six years at various infield positions with the Kenosha Comets and South Bend Blue Sox; Philomena Gianfrancisco and Twila Shively, both of whom played for the Kenosha Comets; pitcher/catcher Irene Kotowicz of the Racine Belles; and Jo Lenard, an all-star who played the infield for nine years with Rockford, Kalamazoo, Peoria, Kenosha, and South Bend. ★

The Places

Home of the Cubs ★★★

In the movie *The Blues Brothers*, Jake and Elwood Blues took advantage of some out-of-towners' ignorance of "Chicahgo's" byways, escaping trouble by giving their home address as 1060 West Addison. Had they tried that trick with a Chicago baseball fan, their blues goose would have been cooked. For that is the street address of not just a ballpark, not just a field, not just a building . . . but a baseball shrine. That is the address of the Friendly Confines of Wrigley Field.

Other than (or perhaps we should say, along with) Fenway Park in Boston, no other ballpark in the majors evokes as much emotion, nostalgia, and as many downright corny reactions as Wrigley. Home to baseball since 1914, it's the second-oldest park in the bigs, but that's not why it is so beloved. Is it the ivy that bedecks its old-time brick outfield walls? Is it the neighborhood, lovingly called Wrigleyville, that surrounds the place? Is it the denizens of the outfield seats, the original "Bleacher Bums"? Or is it the fact that the place is still waiting for another World Series title, nearly a hundred years since its last one in 1908? Probably a combination of all of the above.

While the events on the field, some detailed here and others in the Chicago Cubs chapter, have told one story of Wrigley Field, its creation and subsequent history makes for a pretty good story, too. Though its name evokes a certain chewy confection, it owes its origin to, well, rhubarb pie . . . among other things.

Charles Weeghman was a luncheonette king in pre–World War I Chicago. An innovative gent, he had made fast service, good prices, and comfortable eats a staple on Chi-town street corners. When the Federal League was looking for investors to help them create their rival league (see page 81), Weeghman jumped in with both forks. In 1914, he not only bought the Chicago franchise, he built himself a ballpark. At the time, the South Side was the place to be in Chicago. But Weeghman got a good deal on land up there way above Madison, put up a 16,000-seat park at the cost of $250,000, and ended up attracting 30,000 more fans than the White Sox did that year. But the team that played in this nascent Wrigley was not yet the Cubbies—it was the Whales.

Two years later, that was rectified when the Federal League went under. Knowing a good ballpark when they saw one, and not wanting any other league to get it, the owners of the National League let Weeghman buy the Chicago Cubs and move them into his North Side palace in

1916. Weeghman kept up the innovations, making his place the first to let fans keep foul balls hit into the stands and the first to feature built-in concession stands rather than exclusively roving vendors.

In 1918, business losses forced Weeghman to sell, and the buyer was William Wrigley Jr. Mr. Wrigley was not going to just let his new place go on without some improvements. "I spent $2,300,000 to make Wrigley Field clean, convenient, comfortable, and attractive to the eye," he said. "The effect of these improved surroundings upon baseball patrons has been remarkable." To say the least: He expanded the capacity to more than 35,000 seats, adding more bleachers in the outfield as well as extending the upper decks. And, last but not least, he changed the name of the place to Wrigley Field.

William Wrigley passed his improvement mission on to his son, P. K., who took over after his father died in 1932. P. K. Wrigley set out to make the Cubs' home even more of a showplace (though some would grumble that he paid more attention to the park than the team). In 1937, a key P. K. Wrigley hire, Bill Veeck, permanently changed the character of Wrigley and baseball itself. Though not yet known for the wild stunts of his later years (this was the man who gave baseball the undersized pinch-hitter Eddie Gaedel), Veeck did install Wrigley's famous center-field scoreboard, still hand-operated today. The huge round clock atop the scoreboard went in at the same time. Later that year, P. K. Wrigley ordered Veeck to plant trees to beautify the park. Someone forgot to pass that message on to the fierce Lake Michigan winds and, according to Veeck, the leaves on the trees were stripped in a day. More successful was the installation that season of pots of ivy to grow up the brick outfield wall. That more-hardy plant took root with vigor and today remains Wrigley Field's signature sight. No other park can boast such verdant charms; of course, in no other park can a ball get lost in the ivy (it's a ground-rule double for those of you scoring at home).

So the stage was pretty much set, even before World War II, for a park that would be home to a series of great teams. A wondrous park, covered in ivy, topped by a one-of-a-kind scoreboard, NL team flags fluttering colorfully from its top, and all located in a busy, urban neighborhood of brownstones, shops, and regular people.

Of course, from 1945 onward, it saw exactly zero World Series games. Well, you can't have everything, can you?

Though the Cubbies have yet to bring a title to the ballpark and bars of Wrigleyville, the old place has been the site of numerous moments of baseball legend, among them:

★ **May 2, 1917:** The only double no-hit game in baseball history was pitched. Chicago's Jim "Hippo" Vaughn pitched nine innings without allowing a hit; Cincinnati's Fred Toney did him one better by tossing ten such innings. The Reds won it in the tenth.

★ **October 1, 1932:** Babe Ruth's "called shot." In game three of the 1932 World Series, Ruth stepped up against Chicago's Charlie Root. With two strikes against him, Ruth did something that is debated to this day: he gestured in some fashion. Many contend he was pointing to the center-field seats. Others say he was pointing to Root. Still others say he was motioning to the hecklers on the Cubs' bench. What is not debated is what he did next: wallop a typically Ruthian blast to dead center field. Did he "call" his homer? As Babe once said, "It makes a hell of a story, doesn't it?"

★ **September 28, 1938:** The Homer in the Gloamin'. With darkness (the aforementioned "gloaming") falling and the game tied in a key late-season game against Pittsburgh, catcher Gabby Hartnett slugged a homer that disappeared into the misty twilight. Hartnett touched home, and days later, the Cubs brought home the NL pennant to Wrigley Field.

★ **1945:** The Cubs' last World Series appearance. They lost.

There were also the Cubs' collapses in 1969 and 1984, though those didn't all happen in Wrigley. And in 2003, the world watched in horror—okay, maybe not horror, but then again, not all of us are from Chicago—as Steve Bartman helped craft another chapter in Wrigley's "other" history, the one of failed hopes and dashed chances (again, see the Cubs chapter).

Before Bartman, other than the ivy and Harry Caray, the one thing that Wrigley Field was best known for was the one thing it didn't have: lights. Until 1988, whether Ernie Banks was playing one or two, games were all played under nothing but the sun. Wrigley was the last park in the bigs to add lights and play night baseball. Strangely enough, Wrigley had lights ready to go up before the 1942 season, which would have put them way ahead of the luminosity curve. Construction was set for December 8, 1941. With typical Cubs' luck, following Pearl Harbor, the steel for the light towers was donated to the war effort and the lights stayed out.

The "fight" to add lights to Wrigley was sparked, ironically, by some rare Cubs success. In 1984, the club made the NL Championship Series, one step from the World Series. Though the boys from Wrigley lost, Major League Baseball made it clear that future playoff games involving the Cubbies would be played at night. The team worked for four years to overturn local ordinances against night baseball and to assuage legions of fans who just hated the whole idea of ruining such a long-standing tradition. Finally, on August 8, 1988, the scene was set; lights would, for the first time, brighten a Cubs game at Wrigley. In the long and often sad history of the Cubs, it was to be a momentous event.

Of course, this being the Cubs, it rained. The game was called after three innings.

The lights went on (again) the next night (the Cubs won, defeating the Mets 6–4) and today about a quarter of the team's home games are played under the lights.

Those same neighbors who complained about the addition of Edison's achievement to the Friendly Confines also continue to be among those most devoted to the old park. The Wrigleyville neighborhood surrounding the park adds greatly to its charm. The streets around the place fill with fans on game days—and now nights—packing the bars and creating numerous cottage industries of parking and souvenirs. Another group of economically adventurous fans have taken what used to be a fun (and free) local pastime by turning the roofs of their homes beyond the outfield walls into mini-bleachers. It used to be that you'd get some buddies up there for beer and a barbecue, but ordinances and greed intervened and today it's a booming for-profit business. But a seat across Waveland Avenue behind the right-field wall is still one of the most unique in baseball (as are the crowds that fill the area up the street, waiting for home-run balls to soar over the fence behind the left-field bleachers).

So the old ballpark lives on, conceived in grease and built by gum. Home of baseball's most lovable losers and most devoted fans, site of the fabled ivy and the towering scoreboard, and for the last few years at least, a wonderful place to see a ball game at night.

Jake and Elwood must be very proud of their "home"; stop by next time you're in town. They'll have a cold one waiting . . . and they can leave the lights on. ★

Home of the White Sox ★★★

High above the center-field scoreboard at the home of the 2005 World Champion Chicago White Sox is a sign that reads "U.S. Cellular Field." That's the official name of the park, but c'mon, Chicago, you all know that the White Sox' home field has only one name—let's say it together: "Comiskey Park."

Though the cell phone giant paid a generous sum to the White Sox to name the field, their home will always, to locals, recall that grand old skinflint who ran the team for so many years: Charles Comiskey.

Of course, their current home is actually their second grand baseball palace, and U.S. Cellular was first known as "New Comiskey Park." Here's a look back on the road the ballpark took en route to that happy day when it saw a visit from the World Series Trophy, given to the winner of the annual Fall Classic.

Where It Began

Built in 1910, Comiskey Park was the White Sox' home for eighty years. Named after the Sox' first owner, Charles A. Comiskey, it's the homeland, the mother ship, the place it all began.

Well, kind of. Technically, Comiskey Park was not the team's original home. In 1900, while still a minor-league team, the Sox played at South Side Park, a former cricket field with a capacity of 15,000. But they stayed loyal to their roots for a while, continuing to toss their pitches at South Side Park for a decade.

As the Sox gained popularity those first years, Comiskey saw the need for a larger stadium with more seating and a more fan-friendly atmosphere. To that end, he commissioned architect Zachary Taylor Davis, designer of Wrigley Field, to create the new park with input from himself and his pitching star, Ed Walsh. Perhaps there are some things that were okay to share with the competition.

It wasn't a bad move on Comiskey's part to involve Walsh in the process. But he didn't think about how Walsh might be predisposed to favor a pitcher's park. Walsh advocated for a spacious field of play, with lots of foul territory, and he got it. The field was 362 feet down each line and a whopping 420 feet straightaway to center field. The design was a pitcher's dream perhaps, but a batter's nightmare. For many years, the spacious outfield dimensions would inhibit the team's sluggers.

Comiskey Park opened on July 1, 1910, and the Sox moved into their fancier digs. And so it began: eighty-one years of frustrated batters' complaints.

Growing Up Comiskey

Through the years, Comiskey Park proved it was not impervious to trends. Just as the spectators' attire evolved from knickers to capris, and from bell-bottoms to slacks, Comiskey Park experienced its share of changes to accommodate players and fads. Among the highlights:

★ **1934:** The Sox ownership tried to amend the field's design. Home plate was moved up fourteen feet to accommodate Sox outfielder Al Simmons. When Simmons was traded a year later, the plate was moved back. Easy come, easy go.

★ **1939:** Night baseball was introduced to Chicago at Comiskey Park on August 14. Chicago couples looking for another date spot rejoiced.

★ **1950:** The first large center-field scoreboard was built, replacing the old ones on the left- and right-field walls.

★ **1960:** Bill Veeck introduced an exploding scoreboard, which generated fireworks after each White Sox home run. This lasted until 1982,

when a new scoreboard, complete with a color video screen, was installed.

★ **1968:** Artificial turf was installed on the infield. Player complaints forced its removal in 1976. If it ain't grass, it ain't class.

★ **1990:** All things must come to an end. The White Sox' last game at Comiskey Park was played on September 30, 1990, and was witness to a 2–1 victory over Seattle in the season's final game.

The Games, the Games!

In its lifetime, Comiskey Park was the site of a number of emotional moments, rousing victories, oddball goofs, and history-making games. It hosted the first Major League All-Star Game in 1933. Then, just a few weeks later, Abe Saperstein, owner of the Harlem Globetrotters basketball club and also of the Negro Leagues' Birmingham Black Barons, promoted the first Negro League East-West Game at Comiskey.

Major League Baseball rotated its All-Star Game venues, but Saperstein and other Negro League owners saw no reason to follow their lead. The Negro League East-West Game drew well in Chicago, and so there it remained until 1958.

But the fun didn't end there, and Comiskey Park continued to serve as the birthplace of milestones. On April 16, 1940, Cleveland's Bob Feller threw the only opening day no-hitter in Major League history against the White Sox. Larry Doby, the first African American in the American League, made his debut in Comiskey Park for the Cleveland Indians on July 5, 1947.

On July 11, 1950, the Cardinals' Red Schoendist helped to win the first extra-inning All-Star Game with a fourteenth-inning

home run for a 4-3 win. In the 1983 All-Star Game, the California Angels' Fred Lynn hit the first grand slam in the event's history at Comiskey, helping the American League to a 13–3 win. To top it off, that game also happened to snap an eleven-game losing streak for the American League.

One of the more unusual (or, shall we say, maddening) games at Comiskey transpired on July 1, 1990, when Yankee pitcher Andy Hawkins pitched a complete-game no-hitter but still lost to the White

Sox, 4-0, on five walks and three errors. Just one more opportunity for Sox fans to practice swallowing the bad with the good.

A Turnstile Closes, Another Opens

When Jerry Reinsdorf and Eddie Einhorn took over the Sox in 1980, one of their long-range goals was to build the team a new stadium. Chicagoans can thank tourists for building New Comiskey eleven years later. The $167 million price tag was financed almost entirely by a 2 percent tax charged to guests of city hotels.

New Comiskey Park opened on April 18, 1991, across the street from the old park. It boasted a new exploding scoreboard (of course!), an old-world facade featuring classical brick archways, and more than 40,000 unobstructed-view seats.

Not everyone was happy with tearing down Old Comiskey, but the oldest park in the majors was falling apart. Unfortunately for the White Sox and their fans, the new ballpark was a bit of a hybrid between the all-purpose circular stadiums of the 1960s and what would become the state-of-the-art "modern" ballparks built in places like Cleveland and Baltimore later in the decade. Many fans still mourn the loss of the intimate Old Comiskey and bemoan some of the more antiseptic and less-than-fan-friendly aspects of the new park. Bring a towel for some seats, because nosebleeds are a possibility.

True, the new place does include that exploding scoreboard. The new ballpark was the first in almost twenty years to be built specifically for baseball rather than as a multipurpose venue, and while many Sox fans were unhappy with the demise of the old stadium, the designers stayed true to the memory of the original beloved field. The infield dirt from Comiskey was even transported to New Comiskey's infield.

And for those old-schoolers who want to pay tribute, the original site of Comiskey Park is now marked by a replica home plate and batter's box in the parking lot surrounding the new field.

A record 2,934,154 fans attended games in the stadium's first year. In January of 2003, the White Sox and U.S. Cellular came to a twenty-three-year, $68 million renaming agreement, and the park became U.S. Cellular Field. According to the Sox management, all of the money from the deal would be poured into renovations and improvements to the ballpark. And, true to their word, improvements have been made to create the most family-friendly and fan-enticing atmosphere possible.

U.S. Cellular Field became the first Major League stadium to offer kenneling services for fans' pets. In 2005, the stadium's administration added a three-tier baseball arcade section called FUNdamentals, which features batting cages for kids and radar guns that enable young pitchers to measure the speed of their throws. These features have turned U.S. Cellular into a more child-friendly venue.

The Sox also installed a "Scout Seating" area directly behind home plate. This new 314-seat area allows fans to experience the same angle of action as professional scouts. Fans in this selective area also have access to a 5,000-square-foot private restaurant and lounge.

The craze for new stadiums isn't limited to Chicago. As old, beloved ballparks nationwide are torn down to erect new, high-tech, corporate-sponsored ones, some baseball fans mourn the loss of the historic edifices. Yet, these new stadiums are pulling in record crowds and, ultimately, what matters is that a new generation gets to experience the magic of live baseball. ★

THE TOP TEN

Most Dramatic Moments in Chicago Baseball History ★★★

1. **October 26, 2005.** With two outs in the eighth inning of game four of the World Series, Jermaine Dye drills a single up the middle, scoring pinch-runner Willie Harris to give the White Sox a 1–0 win over the Astros. The win gave Chicago a sweep of the World Series, and the Sox' 11–1 record was one of the most dominant runs through the playoffs since Major League Baseball instituted the three-tier playoff system. With this came an end to almost a century of frustration for White Sox fans. Finally, folks would have something to associate with the Sox other than the 1919 Black Sox scandal.

2. **October 14, 1906.** The White Sox, also known as "the Hitless Wonders" for their inefficiency at the plate that year, stun the cross-town Cubs, 8–3, to win game six of the World Series and close it out. The Sox had been heavy underdogs to a Cubs team that had won 116 games in the regular season, which is still a National League record. Only two other cities have ever hosted a World Series that involved both of the city's Major League clubs: New York has done it several times, and St. Louis did it in 1944 when the Cardinals played the old St. Louis Browns.

3. **October 8, 1908.** The Cubs beat the New York Giants in a one-game playoff for the National League flag—still one of the most dramatic play-offs in baseball history. After tying the Giants for the National League pennant, the Cubs traveled to the Polo Grounds in New York the day after the season ended to settle the question of who would go to the 1908 World Series. In addition, Chicago had to overcome the pitching of Giant ace Christy Mathewson, one of the greatest clutch pitchers of all time. And they did it, winning 4–2. Mordecai "Three Finger" Brown came into the game in the first inning on three days' rest and was the winning pitcher, while Joe Tinker and Frank Chance were the hitting stars. And, oh yes, the Cubs went on to win the World Series—and have yet to claim another title to this day.

4. **September 28, 1938.** Gabby Hartnett hits "the Homer in the Gloamin'." On a very overcast day, the Cubs hosted the Pittsburgh Pirates, whom they led by a half-game in the standings with only a few games left in the season. With the score tied 5–5 in the bottom of the ninth and darkness falling, Cub player-manager Gabby Hartnett took an 0–2 offering from Pirate pitcher Mace Brown and deposited it in the

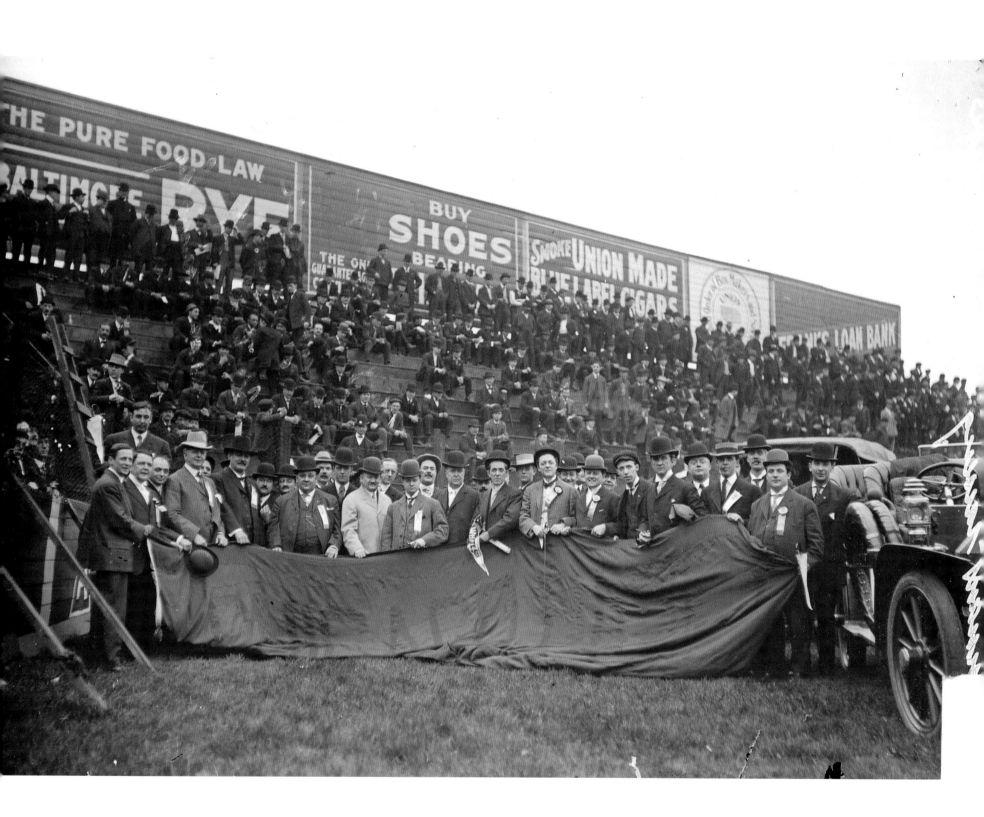

seats. For a moment in the twilight, no one except Hartnett knew the ball was a home run. "I knew it was gone when I hit it," he said. The Cubs won the pennant that year.

5. **October 15, 1917.** The Chicago White Sox defeat the New York Giants 4–2 in game six of the World Series to win their second World Championship. And the long wait for another title began . . .

6. **May 12, 1970.** Ernie Banks hits his five hundredth career home run at Wrigley Field. This was one of the most anticipated events in Cubs history, as fans were eager to honor their beloved star.

7. **August 17, 1990.** Fisk goes deep. White Sox catcher Carlton Fisk belts his 328th home run, setting a new Major League record for home runs by a catcher (since broken by the Mets' Mike Piazza in 2004).

8. **September 13, 1998.** Cubs outfielder Sammy Sosa hits homers number sixty-one and sixty-two. Mark McGwire of the St. Louis Cardinals won the home-run race that year, with seventy to Sosa's sixty-six. But on this evening against the Milwaukee Brewers, Sosa was in the spotlight. He belted a three-run shot in the fifth to tie former Yankee Roger Maris's record, and then in the ninth he cracked a solo blast to break it.

9. **May 6, 1998.** Kerry Wood punches out a score. Wood, a rookie Cub that year, was 2–2 when he took the mound against the Houston Astros. What happened next was a performance for the ages, as Wood struck out twenty batters, with Ricky Gutierrez getting the only Astros hit, in a 2–0 win. Wood became the first National Leaguer to accomplish the feat and the first player ever to strike out his age.

10. **October 23, 2005.** With one out in the bottom of the ninth inning of game two of the World Series, White Sox outfielder Scott Podsednik belts a solo home run—his second of the postseason—to give Chicago a 2–0 lead over the Houston Astros in their best-of-seven series. Podsednik had not hit a single home run in 507 at-bats in the regular season. "It's certainly not what we expected," said Sox first baseman Paul Konerko of Podsednik's blast. ★

THE TOP TEN

Most Disappointing Moments in Chicago Baseball History ★★★

1. **September 29, 1920.** No surprise here. The top spot goes to the Black Sox scandal. Eight members of the 1919 Chicago White Sox are indicted for allegedly conspiring to throw the 1919 World Series against the Cincinnati Reds. The eight are acquitted by a grand jury but are banned from baseball for life by Commissioner Kenesaw Landis. One of the eight was potential Hall of Famer "Shoeless Joe" Jackson.

2. **October 14, 2003.** Leading three games to two, the Cubs battle the Florida Marlins for the National League Championship. But in the eighth inning, Cubs fan Steve Bartman interferes with an attempt by Cubs outfielder Moises Alou to catch a fly ball for the potential second out of the inning. (Television replays make clear that the play is actually not interference.) The Marlins scored eight runs in the frame and rallied to win the National League pennant the next day.

3. **October 1, 1932.** Leading two games to none in the 1932 World Series, the Yankees came to Chicago for game three. As Chicago fans hollered and threw lemons in the fifth inning, Yankee outfielder George Herman "Babe" Ruth pointed at Cubs pitcher Charlie Root.

Root wound up and threw a pitch, and Ruth belted it into the outfield seats for a home run. Although sportswriters insist Ruth pointed to the outfield and, in effect, "called his shot," the facts behind Ruth's gesture will likely never be known. It remains, however, one of the most dramatic home runs in baseball history.

4. **October 8, 1871.** The Great Chicago Fire. Whether Mrs. O'Leary's cow had anything to do with it or not, the fire destroyed the ballpark in which the Chicago White Stockings played, not to mention the team's uniforms and equipment. The White Stockings actually finished the season and ended up in second place, but they were inactive for two years after the fire.

5. **October 10, 1945.** With the World Series against Detroit tied at three games apiece, Cubs manager Charlie Grimm, his pitching staff already thinned out by injury, was looking for a starter. Hank Borowy, who had pitched four relief innings in game six, volunteered. It was a huge mistake. The Tigers hammered Borowy, scored five runs in the first inning, and won the game, 9–3. It was the last time the Cubs were in the World Series.

6. **July 12, 1979.** Disco Demolition Night. Comiskey Park hosted a promotion in which disco records were destroyed in center field. The resulting riot forced the White Sox to forfeit their game to the Detroit Tigers.

7. **October 7, 1984.** After leading two games to none in the National League Championship Series, the Cubs proceeded to lose the next four games to the San Diego Padres. In game five, Chicago started their ace, Rick Sutcliffe. But the Cubs managed only five hits and lost, 6–3.

8. **April 16, 1940.** Bob Feller of the Cleveland Indians threw an opening day no-hitter in Comiskey Park, beating the White Sox 1–0.

9. **October 12, 1929.** Leading 8–0 in game four of the World Series against the Athletics, the Cubs allowed ten runs in the seventh inning to blow the game. Manager Joe McCarthy used four pitchers in the inning, to no avail.

10. **June 18, 1911.** Down 13–1 in the bottom of the sixth inning, the Detroit Tigers made up a twelve-run deficit to stage the biggest comeback in Major League history, eventually beating the White Sox, 16–15. Ty Cobb had five hits and five RBI. The Tigers scored five runs in the eighth and three in the ninth. Sam Crawford's RBI double scored Cobb with the game winner. ★

The People

All-Time All-Stars ★ ★ ★

Over the past century, a couple thousand players have worn the uniforms of the Cubs and the White Sox. Culling twenty-five all-time all-stars for each squad from that many players was not a walk in the park. But if given the opportunity to put them all in the bleachers and pick an all-time all-star team, these would be the guys who would be the elite players for the Cubs and White Sox, respectively.

First Base, Cubs:

★ Cap Anson ★
(1871–1897, Hall of Fame, 1939)

The first player in baseball history to get 3,000 hits, Anson was one of the most durable men in baseball history, playing twenty-seven seasons. He won three batting titles with the Chicago White Stockings, in 1881 and 1888. Anson led the franchise to five pennants.

★ Phil Cavarretta ★
(1934–1955)

A three-time All-Star, Cavarretta was MVP of the National League in 1945, when he led the Cubs to their last World Series appearance. In that Series against the Tigers, he led both teams with a .423 average.

★ Frank Chance ★
(1898–1914, Hall of Fame, 1946)

Called "the Peerless Leader" for his sharp baseball mind and toughness, Chance took the Cubs to four pennants and led the 1908 World Champions with a .421 batting average in the World Series. A superior base stealer, he was the league leader for stolen bases twice.

★ Mark Grace ★
(1988–2003)

The popular Grace was a four-time Gold Glove winner and a three-time All-Star. In 1989, against the Giants in the National League Championship Series, Grace hit a stunning .647 with eleven hits and eight RBI in a losing cause.

Second Base, Cubs:

★ Glenn Beckert ★

(1965–1975)

This four-time All-Star was also a Gold Glove second baseman in 1968. An excellent contact hitter, Beckert was tough to strike out. In 1968, he struck out only twenty times in 643 at-bats.

★ Johnny Evers ★

(1902–1917, 1922, Hall of Fame, 1946)

Called "the Crab" for the sideways manner in which he played ground balls, Evers was a superb defensive player. While high-strung and combative, he played in four World Series and hit .350 or better in three of them.

★ Billy Herman ★

(1931–1947, Hall of Fame, 1975)

William Jennings Bryan Herman was one of the top second basemen of the 1930s and early 1940s. A ten-time All-Star, Herman hit .300 or better eight times in his career and scored at least 100 runs five times.

★ Ryne Sandberg ★

(1981–1997, Hall of Fame, 2005)

"Ryno," as Cubs fans called him, was the most celebrated second baseman the franchise ever had. A ten-time All-Star, he won nine Gold Gloves and was National League MVP in 1984.

Third Base, Cubs:

★ Stan Hack ★

(1932-1947)

The affable Hack, nicknamed "Smilin' Stan" for his perpetual grin, was a defensive marvel for Chicago. A four-time All-Star who twice led the

National League in fielding and five times in putouts, Hack also scored 100 or more runs seven times in his seventeen years of play.

★ Ron Santo ★

(1960–1974)

Santo was a nine-time All-Star and a five-time Gold Glove Award winner. Though not a flashy player, he was one of the best players of the 1960s and many believe that he should be in the Hall of Fame.

Shortstop, Cubs:

★ Ernie Banks ★

(1954–1971, Hall of Fame, 1977)

The foremost player in Cubs history and maybe in Chicago baseball history, "Mr. Cub," as he was known, was an eleven-time All-Star and was MVP in 1958 and again in 1959. From 1955 to 1960, Banks hit more home runs than anyone else in baseball, including Mickey Mantle, Willie Mays, and Hank Aaron.

★ Don Kessinger ★

(1964–1979)

A six-time All-Star for the Cubs, a solid defender and pesky hitter who once went 6-for-6 in a ten-inning game. In 1969, he played fifty-four consecutive games at shortstop without an error, then a National League record.

Outfield, Cubs:

★ Andre Dawson ★

(1976-1996)

"The Hawk," as he was called, was an eight-time All-Star with Montreal and the Cubs. The eight-time Gold Glove Award winner was also MVP in 1987, when he hit a league-best forty-nine homers and added 137 RBI for the Cubbies.

★ Andy Pafko ★

(1943–1959)

"Handy Andy" Pafko, a four-time All-Star, was given his nickname by Cubs manager Charlie Grimm, who often used Pafko at third base as well as in the outfield. He also hit .300 or better three times as a Cub.

★ Sammy Sosa ★

(1989–2004)

Sosa lost the home-run title in 1998 to Mark McGwire but still won the MVP award—and deservedly so, as he led the Cubs to the postseason that year. The six-time All-Star came back to hit sixty-three dingers the next season, proving he was no statistical fluke.

★ Hack Wilson ★

(1923–1934, Hall of Fame, 1979)

Lewis Robert "Hack" Wilson was not a big man at 5'6", but he could pound the ball. Wilson remains the big-league record holder in RBI with 191 and, until McGwire's seventy in 1998, was the National League home-run king with fifty-six in the 1930 season.

★ Billy Williams ★

(1959–1976, Hall of Fame, 1987)

The smooth-swinging Williams was a hitting machine. The 1972 batting champion was the 1961 Rookie of the Year, as well as a four-time All-Star. From September 22, 1963, to September 2, 1970, he established a National League record with 1,117 consecutive games played, a mark later broken by the Dodgers' Steve Garvey.

Opposite: *Charles "Gabby" Hartnett was an all-star catcher for the Cubs for twenty years. Right: Michael "King" Kelly strikes a cocky pose in 1887 as a member of the Boston Beaneaters.*

Catcher, Cubs:

★ Gabby Hartnett ★

(1922–1941, Hall of Fame, 1955)

Charles Leo "Gabby" Hartnett was given his nickname by teammates who chuckled at Hartnett's shy ways. But Hartnett let his play do the talking: he was league MVP in 1935 and a six-time All-Star.

★ King Kelly ★

(1878–1893, Hall of Fame, 1945)

Michael Joseph "King" Kelly may have been the best player of the nineteenth century, and that includes Cap Anson. Kelly could play any position and was a two-time batting champion in 1884 and 1886. He hit .300 or better eight times and led his teams to eight championships in his sixteen seasons of play.

Pitcher, Cubs:

★ Mordecai Brown ★

(1903–1916, Hall of Fame, 1949)

Brown was the most effective "money pitcher" in team history, with a 5–4 record in the World Series and a 2.97 ERA. Brown was the winning pitcher in the tension-packed 1908 playoff game against the New York Giants.

Big Lee Smith prepares to snap off a heater for Chicago.

★ John Clarkson ★

(1882, 1884–1894, Hall of Fame, 1963)

Clarkson won twenty or more games for eight consecutive seasons, from 1885 to 1892, and was among the league leaders in strikeouts, shutouts, and ERA in that span. He was also one of the best fielders of his era.

★ Ferguson Jenkins ★

(1965–1983)

Jenkins had an amazing six consecutive twenty-win seasons with the Cubs, from 1967 to 1972, and won the Cy Young Award in 1971. He threw more than 300 innings in a season five times and struck out over 3,100 batters in his career.

★ Greg Maddux ★

(1986–present)

"Mad Dog" made his debut in 1986 and won the Cy Young Award in 1992. Unfortunately for the Cubs, he left the team via free agency after that season and played his prime years for the Atlanta Braves, where he won three more Cy Youngs and a World Series ring. He returned to play for the Cubs in 2004 and won his 300th career game that season.

★ Lee Smith ★

(1980–1997)

The imposing (6'6", 240 pounds) Smith led the league in saves four times in his career and was named to the All-Star team seven times. His 478 saves is still the all-time record.

★ Lon Warneke ★

(1930–1943)

"The Arkansas Hummingbird" got his unique nickname because he was a talented singer and expert ukulele player. He also was a five-time All-Star who helped the Cubs win the 1932 and 1935 National League pennants.

First Base, White Sox:

★ Dick Allen ★

(1963–1977)

Enigmatic but undeniably talented, Dick Allen had a lightning-fast swing and power to spare. He led the league with thirty-seven homers and 113 RBI in 1972, earning him the MVP. Two years later, he won the home-run crown again with thirty-two dingers.

★ Frank Thomas ★

(1990–present)

"The Big Hurt," as Thomas is known, is a two-time MVP with the White Sox, in 1993 and 1994. At the end of the 2005 season, Thomas's 448 home runs placed him first in franchise history. His 1,466 walks are seventeenth best in Major League history.

Second Base, White Sox:

★ Eddie Collins ★

(1906–1930, Hall of Fame, 1939)

Collins was one of the most skilled all-around players in the history of the game. He led the league in stolen bases three times and in runs scored four times. While there were no All-Star teams in Collins's era, he was without a doubt the preeminent second baseman of his day.

★ Nellie Fox ★

(1947–1965, Hall of Fame, 1997)

Fox was an eleven-time All-Star and three-time Gold Glove Award winner who was the heart and soul of the Sox for fourteen seasons. He hit .300 or better six times and was very tough to strike out, whiffing only 216 times in 9,232 career at-bats.

Shortstop, White Sox:

★ Luis Aparicio ★

(1956–1973, Hall of Fame, 1984)

Playing alongside Nellie Fox in the late 1950s and early 1960s, Aparicio helped form one of the smoothest-fielding combinations in baseball history. A seven-time All-Star, Aparicio also won nine Gold Gloves. When he retired, he ranked seventh on the all-time list with 506 stolen bases.

★ Luke Appling ★

(1930–1943, 1945–1950, Hall of Fame, 1964)

Another player with a great nickname, "Old Aches and Pains" was constantly complaining about injuries, both real and imagined. Still, Appling was an eight-time All-Star and won the first-ever batting title by a White Sox ballplayer in 1936 with a .388 average.

★ Chico Carrasquel ★

(1950–1959)

Alfonso "Chico" Carrasquel had a strong first season, hitting .282 with a twenty-four-game hitting streak as a rookie. The four-time All-Star broke an American League record by accepting 297 chances in fifty-three games without an error in 1951.

★ Ozzie Guillen ★

(1985–2000)

Guillen came onto the scene with a bang, winning the Rookie of the Year Award in 1985 and leading the league in fielding percentage with a .980 mark. The two-time All-Star also hit twenty or more doubles seven times in his career. In 2004, he was hired as the White Sox' manager; he led them to the World Series title in 2005.

Third Base, White Sox:

★ Bill Melton ★

(1968–1977)

Melton led the league in home runs in 1971 with thirty-three while playing for Chicago and was the first Sox player to win a home-run crown. The powerful Melton was a good, but not great, fielder and often drew the ire of Sox broadcaster Harry Caray after making an error.

★ Buck Weaver ★

(1912–1920)

George "Buck" Weaver was such a terrific defensive third baseman that Ty Cobb reportedly refused to bunt on him. Possessed of a powerful arm, he was also a tough clutch hitter, socking .327 in two World Series. Weaver reportedly did not agree to throw the 1919 Series, but knew about the plot and was thrown out of baseball with seven other teammates.

Catcher, White Sox:

★ Carlton Fisk ★

(1969–1993, Hall of Fame, 2000)

The New Hampshire–born Fisk was a Boston Red Sox favorite until he was whisked away to Chicago in 1981. The eleven-time All-Star was also popular in Chicago and was renowned as an excellent handler of pitchers. Fisk retired as the all-time home-run leader for catchers with 376. The 1972 Rookie of the Year also won a Gold Glove in 1973.

★ Ray Schalk ★

(1912–1929, Hall of Fame, 1955)

Schalk caught a record four no-hitters in his career and caught 100 or more games twelve times in his career. An innovator, Schalk was reportedly the first catcher to back up plays at first and third base. Schalk led the league in fielding as a catcher eight times in his career.

Outfield, White Sox:

★ Harold Baines ★

(1980–2000)

A six-time All-Star, Baines led the Sox in slugging percentage in 1984 with a .571 average. The soft-spoken Baines, whose one-legged batting style reminded many of Mel Ott, led the American League in 1983 with twenty-two game-winning RBI. Baines hit twenty or more homers in six consecutive seasons for Chicago.

★ Joe Jackson ★

(1908–1920)

"Shoeless Joe" was so nicknamed because he once played a semipro game in his stocking feet. He was considered the best natural hitter of his era. His .356 career average is still third best all time behind Ty Cobb and Rogers Hornsby. He hit .375 in the 1919 World Series to lead both teams, but he took money from gamblers, which got him and seven teammates banned from the game for life.

Opposite: *Feisty Ray Schalk was one of the best defensive catchers of his era. Schalk was another player trying to win the 1919 World Series, hitting .304 in eight games. He was elected to the Hall of Fame in 1955.* Right: *Magglio Ordonez takes a cut in a game in April 14, 2004, against the Royals at U.S. Cellular Field. The Sox won the game, 10–9.*

★ Minnie Minoso ★

(1949, 1951–1964, 1976, 1980)

Orestes "Minnie" Minoso debuted in 1949 but was still a rookie when he was obtained by the White Sox in 1951, becoming the first black player in the team's history. He lost the Rookie of the Year award, leading the league with thirty-one stolen bases and fourteen triples. Minoso was a seven-time All-Star and a three-time Gold Glove winner.

★ Magglio Ordonez ★

(1997–2004)

Ordonez was a four-time All-Star with the White Sox and hit .300 or better in six of his eight seasons with Chicago. In 2002, he was second in the league with 135 RBI and added a .320 batting average, good for fifth overall. He signed with the Detroit Tigers as a free agent after the 2004 season.

Pitcher, White Sox:

★ Eddie Cicotte ★

(1905, 1908–1920)

Cicotte was another member of the 1919 Black Sox, along with Joe Jackson, who threw away a Hall of Fame career. He won twenty or more games three times in his career, including a league-leading twenty-eight in 1919. His all-time record was 208–149.

★ Red Faber ★

(1914–1933, Hall of Fame, 1964)

Urban Clarence "Red" Faber was so named for his reddish hair. He pitched in Chicago his entire career, and while many of those years were with sub-.500 clubs, he won more games than he lost, including ten consecutive years (1914–1923) with a winning record.

★ Ted Lyons ★

(1923–1942, 1946, Hall of Fame, 1955)

Like Faber, Lyons also pitched in Chicago his entire career, winning 260 games. Lyons never pitched in the minor leagues and never pitched in the postseason, but he was a real competitor. Lyons played for mostly sub-.500 teams but still won more than he lost most years. An excellent control pitcher, he once went forty-two consecutive innings without issuing a base on balls.

★ Jack McDowell ★

(1987–1999)

"Black Jack" McDowell spent seven of his twelve Major League years with the Sox. He was a three-time All-Star with Chicago and won twenty or more games twice. McDowell also led the league in complete games twice, with fifteen in 1991 and thirteen in 1992.

★ Billy Pierce ★

(1945, 1948–1964)

Pierce was the ace of the Sox staff for much of the 1950s and early 1960s. He threw four one-hitters and was a seven-time All-Star. A competitor who wanted the ball, Pierce matched up against Yankees ace Whitey Ford and won ten of eighteen decisions. He was also 7–2 against Cleveland ace Bob Lemon.

★ Ed Walsh ★

(1904–1917, Hall of Fame, 1946)

"Big Ed" Walsh was the White Sox pitching mainstay at the turn of the century. In 1908, Big Ed threw an astonishing 464 innings and won forty games. No pitcher has topped that since. Walsh was another spitball pitcher but had a number of other pitches to mix in. His career ERA of 1.82 is one of the lowest of all time.

★ Doc White ★

(1901–1913)

Guy Harris "Doc" White was a graduate of dental school at Georgetown, hence his nickname. He was a key pitcher for the Sox in the early part of the twentieth century and in 1906 was 18–6 with a league-best 1.82 ERA. In 1907, he won a league-high twenty-seven games.

★ Hoyt Wilhelm ★

(1952–1972, Hall of Fame, 1985)

A master of the knuckleball, Wilhelm appeared in more games (1,071) than any other pitcher in Major League history, except for Dennis Eckersley and Jesse Orosco. He established records, since broken, in relief wins (123) and games pitched in relief (1,018). Wilhelm was the first reliever to be elected to the Hall of Fame.

★ Wilbur Wood ★

(1961–1965, 1967–1978)

The rubber-armed Wood was, like his teammate Wilhelm, a workhorse. He led the American League in relief appearances from 1968 to 1970 but in 1971 was turned into a starter. Frequently pitching on only two days' rest, Wood won twenty or more games for four consecutive years. He started both games of a doubleheader in 1973 but was hit hard in both games by the Yankees. ★

HOMETOWN HEROES:
The Minors ★★★

Chicago has always been a big-league town, so while there are few memorable minor-league moments within its boundaries, a number of Chicago-born players made their marks in the minor leagues elsewhere. Many listed here played in the early part of the twentieth century, when long minor-league careers were common and a player could make a very good living playing minor-league ball.

Born in Chicago, **Jack Lelivelt** played parts of six years in the Major Leagues, from 1909 to 1914, but the vast majority of his career was spent at the minor-league level. In all, he played part or all of nineteen years in the minors (1906 to 1931), compiling a .331 batting average.

His best year was in 1921, as a first baseman for Omaha of the Western League. He won the batting title with a .416 average, with seventy doubles and 274 hits, both league bests. He also had fourteen homers and twenty-four stolen bases. Those seventy doubles were a professional record at the time, the most in both the majors and the minors.

Lelivelt was also a crackerjack manager. In a twenty-one-year career (1920 to 1940), he managed six different teams in three different minor leagues, winning eight pennants and finishing second four times.

One of the most legendary ballplayers to come out of Chicago was **Alexander A. "Duke" Reilley**, also known as "Midget" because of his 5'4", 145-pound frame. Signed in 1905 by Erie of the Inter-State League as a twenty-one-year-old, the Duke spent nineteen years in the minors.

A good bunter and a clever base stealer, Reilley hit .313 and played the outfield. He led the Ohio State League in steals in 1908 and 1909, with eighty and seventy-six swipes, respectively. Ten times he stole more than thirty bases in a season, five times more than forty.

Reilley was called up to the Show in 1920; he played twenty games for Cleveland and hit .210.

Sheldon LeJeune didn't like his given name, so he asked his friends and teammates to call him "Larry." LeJeune by any name could hit—at least in the minors. He won five batting titles in his ten-year minor-league career that began in 1907 with Springfield, Illinois, of the Central League. In 1912, LeJeune won the title with a .361 average and led the league with 168 hits, forty-nine stolen bases, and twenty-five home runs.

LeJeune spent six games with the Brooklyn Dodgers in 1911, hitting .158, and eighteen games with the Pittsburgh Pirates in 1915, hitting .169.

Philip Weintraub had a decent major-league career, playing parts of seven years with the Reds, Giants, and the Phillies. He hit .295 in 444 games in the bigs. But Weintraub spent sixteen years in the minors, with fifteen different teams, from 1930 to 1945. A muscular 6'1", 195 pounds, Weintraub could hit. He batted over .300 in eleven of those fifteen seasons and won the batting crown of the Southern League in 1934 with a .401 average.

The two best minor-league pitchers of Chicago were righty **Frank Dasso** and left-hander **Walter Leverenz**.

Dasso began his career in 1936 with Canton of the Mid-Atlantic League, going 4–7 as a raw nineteen-year-old. But he went on to pitch in the minors for eighteen years, winning 175 games and losing 200.

Leverenz spent twenty-two years in the minors, with a brief two-and-a-half-year major-league stint with the St. Louis Browns from 1913 to 1915, where he went 7–31.

In his stellar minor-league career, he won twenty or more games three times, and from 1917 to 1925 he won eleven or more games. He was 269–228 in the minors.

Two other Chicago-born managers are of note. **Stanley Wasiak** managed from 1950 to 1986, winning 2,570 games. He won five pennants in his career, including a third-place finish in 1959 with Green Bay of the Three-I League, where he went 35–27 to finish third but won the playoff for the title.

Spencer Abbot managed twenty-four different clubs from 1903 to 1947 (not consecutively—Abbot missed several years to both World War I and World War II). Abbot was reportedly from the John McGraw school of "win at all costs" and was not always popular with owners or players. Often fired but always in demand, he won four pennants in four different leagues, and his all-time record was 2,180–2,037. ★

Hometown Heroes:
Chicago-Born Major Leaguers ★★★

In addition to Hall of Famer Charlie Comiskey, there have been a host of Chicagoans who have made their mark in other cities. There are more than eighty Chicago-based big-leaguers, but these ballplayers with extended careers have earned spots on our mythical All-Chicago squad. Honorable mention goes to Chicagoan **Earl Pruess**, who played one game for the 1920 St. Louis Browns, pinch-hitting in the eighth inning. He walked in his only at-bat, stole second, and scored on a base hit. He then took the outfield, catching two fly balls for outs. His on-base percentage, fielding average, and stolen-base percentage were all 1.000. If you only get to play one game in the big leagues, you might as well be perfect.

Dick "Rowdy Richard" Bartell played shortstop and third base for the Pirates, Phillies, Giants, Cubs, and Tigers. Bartell had a batting average of .300 or better six times in an eighteen-year career (1927 to 1946) and hit .294 in three World Series. His nickname derived from his combative nature.

Wally Berger played from 1930 to 1940. Ironically, he was originally the property of the Cubs but was traded to the Boston Braves prior to the 1930 season. Powerfully built and blessed with a good eye for pitches, Berger hit .300 or better in four of his first seven years with the Braves. He topped thirty homers three times, leading the National League in 1935 with an impressive thirty-four. After seven solid years in Boston, Berger bounced around the league, playing with the Giants, Reds, and Phillies in the last four years of career.

Oswald Lewis "Ossie" Bluege was one of the best third basemen in the American League in the 1920s. He played his entire career, from 1922 to 1939, with the Senators. Solid and unspectacular yet incredibly consistent, Bluege never put up big numbers but always played well under pressure. A company man for the Senators for most of his life, he served them as a coach (1940 to 1942), manager (1943 to 1947), and farm director (1948 to 1956). An accountant in the off-season, Bluege was the comptroller for the club from 1957 to 1971.

"Big Jim" Clancy pitched for the Toronto Blue Jays for twelve of the fifteen years he was in the majors, 1977 to 1991. Clancy toiled for some wretched Blue Jay squads, although he was never far from the

.500 mark. In 1982, he made the All-Star team with a 16–14 record and an ERA of 3.71. He spent his last three years with the Houston Astros. Clancy's lifetime record was 140–167.

Frederick "Cy" Falkenberg was a journeyman pitcher for the Pirates, Senators, and Indians when he was signed to a big contract with Indianapolis of the outlaw Federal League in 1914. Falkenberg became a star for Indy, going 25–16 with 236 strikeouts and nine shutouts, as he led his team to the first Federal League pennant. With winning seasons in only seven of his twelve years in the majors, Falkenberg played from 1903 to 1917 and had a 131–123 record.

Charles "Chick" Fraser was a wiry hurler who pitched for seven teams in a fourteen-year career from 1896 to 1909. Fraser threw a no-hitter for the Phillies in 1903 and twice won twenty or more games in his career. But he also lost twenty or more games five times. Fraser led the league in walks three times, as well, once giving away 166 free passes for Louisville his rookie year. At 175–212, Fraser is the winningest—and losingest—Chicago-born pitcher in major-league history.

Johnny Groth had a spectacular rookie year with the Detroit Tigers as the team's regular center fielder in 1949, hitting .293 with eleven homers and seventy-three RBI. He returned the next year to hit .306. Following a trade to the St. Louis Browns in 1953, Groth's production dropped. He played ten more years in the majors but never recaptured the production of those first two seasons.

Rickey Henderson had one of the longest and most productive careers of any Major Leaguer in recent memory. He played twenty-five years in the big leagues, mostly in the outfield, from 1979 to 2003.

Henderson, also known as "the Man of Steal," played for, in order: Oakland, the New York Yankees, Oakland again, Toronto, Oakland yet again, San Diego, Anaheim, Oakland a fourth time, the New York Mets,

Seattle, San Diego again, Boston, and the Los Angeles Dodgers. He is one of the greatest leadoff hitters in baseball history. The 1990 American League MVP was a ten-time All-Star and is the all-time leader in runs scored, with 2,295. His career record of 1,406 stolen bases is unlikely to be broken, and he is also second on the all-time list in walks, with 2,190.

Left-hander **Charlie Leibrandt** was a consistently solid starter for the Royals in the mid-1980s. In the 1985 World Series, he pitched seven scoreless innings in game six to help give Kansas City a 2–1 win and square the Series. The Royals won the World Championship the next night, 11–0. Leibrandt never won twenty games in his career, which lasted from 1979 to 1993, but he ended up 140–119.

Freddie Lindstrom is already in the Hall of Fame, having been elected in 1976. He played most of his thirteen-year career (1924 to 1936) with the Giants, with brief stints with the Pirates, Cubs, and Dodgers at the end of his career.

Lindstrom hit .300 or better in seven of his thirteen seasons, including a .358 mark with 231 hits and 107 RBI in 1928. He was a third baseman for the first half of his career, but back troubles eventually moved him to the outfield.

Herman Long was one of the best shortstops in the majors in the nineteenth century and should probably be a Hall of Famer himself. Long played from 1889 to 1903 and was known as "the Flying Dutchman" before that nickname was bestowed upon Honus Wagner. Long led the league in runs scored with 149 in 1893. He anchored a powerful Boston Beaneaters infield in the 1890s, leading the squad to five National League pennants. His 6.4 chances per game converted remains the best career mark in the major leagues.

Long was abrasive, tough, and played for keeps at all times. In 1892, he broke catcher Connie Mack's leg on a hard slide into home, despite the fact that there was no play at the plate.

Greg Luzinski, also known as "the Bull," played a few years with the White Sox at the end of his career but was better known as a slugger for the Philadelphia Phillies. Luzinski, a four-time All-Star, played from 1970 to 1984. His best year was 1977, when he hit thirty-nine home runs and added 130 RBI to go with a .309 batting average.

The Phillies of the 1970s reached the postseason three times with Luzinski on the roster, but the year they won the World Series, 1980, Luzinski was injured and did not get a hit in the Fall Classic. Luzinski was traded to the White Sox prior to the 1981 season, and the Sox used him primarily as a designated hitter.

Fred Lynn is associated with either Boston or the West Coast in the minds of many baseball fans, but he was born in Chicago in 1952. In 1975 with the Red Sox, Lynn had one of the greatest rookie seasons of any player in the history of baseball, hitting .331 with twenty-one homers and a league-leading forty-seven doubles and 103 runs scored. The Red Sox made it to the World Series that year, and Lynn was the first player in major-league history to be named Rookie of the Year and league MVP in the same season.

Yet that monster season turned out to be something of a curse. Lynn hit twenty or more home runs nine more times, made ten All-Star teams, won the batting title in 1979 for Boston with a .333 average,

and had several strong seasons. Unfortunately, nothing compared to his 1975 season. Lynn was an excellent all-around player who went all-out. This sometimes resulted in injuries, and although he played seventeen years, he was sidelined with injuries all too often.

Denny McLain is remembered only for his amazing 1968 season, when he went 31–6 with a league-leading twenty-eight complete games, 336 innings pitched to go with 280 strikeouts, and six shutouts. But McLain won twenty or more games two other times, in 1966 and 1969, and was 131–91 lifetime. After winning the Cy Young award in 1968, he came back in 1969 with a 24–9 mark and tied for it again.

McLain was a national figure during 1968, appearing on *The Ed Sullivan Show* and at various Las Vegas casinos. He was absent from the team so often, flying here and there, that he was nicknamed "Sky King." But it all unraveled in 1970. He clashed with the Tiger ownership, fell to 3–5, and was traded to the Washington Senators. McLain dropped to 10–22 there, and within two years, at age twenty-eight, he was out of baseball.

Marty McManus spent the first part of his career as a utility player, appearing at all four infield positions for the St. Louis Browns. Primarily a second baseman, McManus was a contact hitter and a good base runner. He led the league in stolen bases with twenty-three in 1930, and his forty-four doubles in 1925 also topped the circuit.

After a stint with the Tigers, McManus was player-coach with the awful Boston Red Sox from 1931 to 1933 and then finished his career, which lasted from 1913 to 1928, with the crosstown Braves.

Fred "Fritz" Peterson toiled for the New York Yankees during their doldrum years of the late 1960s to early 1970s. Yet despite playing for ordinary Yankee squads, the left-handed pitcher won twenty games in 1970 and seventeen in 1972. Peterson ended up 133–131 for his career, which ran from 1966 to 1976.

Wally Pipp is best known for losing his first baseman's job to Lou Gehrig, but he was also a terrific first baseman in his own right. Pipp played for New York for eleven years, appeared in three World Series, and led the league in home runs in 1916 and again in 1917.

A slick-fielding first baseman who could also run the base paths, he led the league in triples with nineteen in 1925.

The real story of his benching is that he simply wasn't playing well, and manager Miller Huggins wanted to work Gehrig into the lineup. Gehrig took the job away from Pipp in 1925 and never gave it up. Pipp was traded to the Reds and played three more years.

Kirby Puckett played his entire twelve-year career, which lasted from 1984 to 1995, with the Minnesota Twins, and is one of the most popular players in their history. At 5'8", 220 pounds, he was built like a potato but hit like a wrecking ball.

Puckett was a ten-time All-Star, a six-time Gold Glove winner in the outfield, and the MVP of the 1993 All-Star game, hitting a double and a homer in an American League win. He also led the Twins to World Series wins in 1987 and 1991, over the Cardinals and Braves, respectively. In the 1991 American League Championship Series win over Toronto, Puckett hit .429 with a double, two homers, and six RBI.

In 2001, Puckett was inducted into the Hall of Fame.

Doug Rader played eleven years in the bigs, from 1967 to 1977, mostly with the Houston Astros, mostly at third base. Rader, called "the Red Rooster" for his hair-trigger temper, was a good-fielding, average-hitting infielder for the Astros in their early years. His best year was 1974, when he hit .257 with a career-best twenty-seven doubles.

William "Moose" Skowron was a mainstay at first base for the New York Yankees from 1954 to 1962, when he was traded to the Los Angeles Dodgers. Skowron hit .300 or better six times in that span. But his forte was the postseason. Skowron hit .293 in thirty-five games with New York and four with the Dodgers. He had eight postseason home runs and twenty-nine RBI. When he was traded to the Dodgers, he responded by hitting .385 with a home run in the Dodgers' four-game sweep of Skowron's old team.

"Moose" (short for Mussolini, a childhood nickname) was traded to the White Sox in 1964, and played for his hometown team until 1967, when, after a brief stint with the Angels, he retired.

The speedy **Lonnie Smith** spent seventeen years (1978 to 1994) in the bigs with six teams, four of whom he helped into the World Series. Smith stole twenty or more bases eight times in his career, batted over .300 six times, and was an All-Star in 1982.

His postseason success was memorable. He helped the Philadelphia Phillies to a World Championship in 1980 and the St. Louis Cardinals to the title in 1982, and in 1985, he was a midseason pickup by the Kansas City Royals. Smith responded by hitting .333 to win his third World Series with a different team.

Milt Stock spent all fourteen years of his career (1913 to 1926) in the National League, with the Giants, Phillies, Cardinals, and Dodgers. The diminutive (5'4", 163 pounds) Stock was a tough-as-nails third baseman who hit better than .300 six times.

Kirby Puckett, Fred Lynn, Rickey Henderson, Greg Luzinski. One sort of wishes they could have stayed closer to home. The 1983 White Sox with Lynn would have been a nice combination, and who knows what would have happened if Rickey Henderson had played for the 1989 Cubs? What this chapter does illustrate is the quality of Chicago-born ballplayers and the rich tradition of the game in the city. ★

The Broadcasters ★ ★ ★

One of the best things about Chicago baseball is the two pro teams' roster of Hall of Fame announcers. Perhaps only New York can boast of as many legendary voices as Chicago. Name a baseball voice from Seattle. How about Boston? Cleveland? Los Angeles? Okay, that last one's Vin Scully. But the Dodgers are better known than Scully. The same might not always be said of Harry Caray and the Cubs. No baseball broadcaster in the last half-century has been as identified with his team, or as nationally famous, as Caray was for the Cubs. But what is most truly "Chicago" about him is that before he joined the Cubs in 1982, he had been with the White Sox since 1969! That's like working at the White House and then moving to Cuba (or vice versa, depending on where you live in Chicago).

But working for multiple teams was nothing new in Chicago. The equally legendary, if less wacky, Jack Brickhouse had not only worked for the Cubs for decades, he also had worked White Sox games—often working both jobs in the same season. Try that today and you'd get laughed out of the production truck.

Old-time Cubs fans, however, swear that it is the stentorian tones of Jack Brickhouse that remain the standard for all broadcasters. Brickhouse, who began his broadcasting career at age eighteen at a radio station in Peoria, was hired by the White Sox in 1940 and by the Cubs in 1941. He broadcast games for both franchises for several decades. Cubs and White Sox fans grew up listening to Brickhouse, who was a pro's pro. Fans recall that one of his great attributes was that he didn't feel the need to clutter up the airwaves.

Rounding out the all-stars who also held allegiances to both Chicago teams was Bob Elson. One of the Cubs' earliest broadcasters, "the Old Commander" was hired by the Cubs in 1928 and stayed with the club for over a decade. Even despite this long service, Elson is best known for his work with the White Sox, whose games he announced from 1944 to 1970. In 1945, two legends combined when he and Brickhouse were paired as a broadcasting team for the White Sox on WJJD radio.

Brickhouse, Elson, and Caray are the holy trinity of Chicago media. All three have been honored by the Baseball Hall of Fame as winners of the Ford C. Frick broadcasting award. But of the three, Harry Caray remains the closest to fans' hearts.

The Caray Legend

Caray started his career in the early 1970s broadcasting White Sox games with Ralph Faucher at radio station WTAQ. He stayed with the Sox until 1982 before joining the Cubs for the most high-profile part of his career.

Even though Harry's gone to the big booth in the sky, he's still with fans at every Cubs game. The tradition he started, singing "Take Me Out to the Ball Game" during the seventh-inning stretch from his booth behind home plate, has continued to this day. At each home game, a local or national celebrity attempts, often vainly but usually with great good humor, to mimic Harry. But though Will Ferrell tried it on *Saturday Night Live* and every Chicago comic gives it their best shot, no one can truly imitate Harry. No announcer loved his home team more, none were quicker to praise, and few were quicker to criticize. Harry was always one of us, just a bleacher bum who had been handed a mic.

Those enormous glasses, that bombastic voice, that wandering story line, the occasional gaffe—all were part of his charm. He is credited with the famous shout "Cubs win! Cubs win!" after Chicago victories. When he died in 1998 (just one year after he left his Cubs), the entire city mourned, and his funeral was a citywide wake. The team wore an arm patch on their sleeves the entire next season. That's love, folks, and for a guy who just talked for a living.

Was Caray bigger than the Cubs? Well, yes, probably. But then again, when your team loses year after year, you've got to look for the bright spots, and to do that, Cubs fans all looked up behind home plate for the guy in the big specs.

In the Shadow of Legends

Caray was paired with some interesting broadcast partners in his tenure. From 1977 to 1981, his color man was former Red Sox outfielder

Jimmy Piersall, whose antics as a player included throwing a ball at the exploding scoreboard after a home run at Comiskey Park.

But Piersall's outspokenness was his downfall as a broadcaster. He was fired in 1981 for being critical of the Cubs' management.

The longest-tenured broadcaster presently working in Chicago is former third baseman Ron Santo, hired by the Cubs in 1990. Santo's radio broadcasts didn't go over well initially, but his hard work over the past decade has paid off, and he's now a great crowd favorite.

But no story about Chicago broadcasters would be complete without the tale of Ronald "Dutch" Reagan (yes, the very same), who broadcast Cubs games for radio station WHO in Iowa from 1933 to 1936.

Actually, what Reagan broadcast were "re-creations" of Cubs games from his booth in Iowa—a common practice in the 1930s, when remote broadcasts were technical nightmares. Reagan would get batter-by-batter results and relay them to his listeners. By most accounts, Dutch was pretty good. However, he wanted to pursue an acting career and left radio in 1936. Turns out he had even higher aspirations . . .

Brickhouse, Elson, Caray, Reagan, Santo, Piersall . . . these were the people who brought the Cubs and the Sox into living rooms and exponentially expanded the teams' fan bases. In fact, these radio and television broadcasters are credited by some baseball historians as the reason why both teams, despite often terrible records, have gained followings of such intense fans over the years. ★

The Fans ★ ★ ★

Madison Avenue slices straight as a line drive through the heart of Chicago, sticking out from Lake Michigan like a demarcation line. North of the line: Cubs fans, Wrigleyville, a "curse," and Harry Caray. South of the line: White Sox fans, Old and New Comiskeys, exploding scoreboards, and Harry Caray. That Harry got around, of course (see page 156), but the point is that Chicago is a two-team baseball city, the oldest such toddlin' town in the bigs. For more than a hundred years, Chicago fans have had a simple choice: Cubs or Sox. You don't get to pick both. There are no diplomats in foxholes.

The fans of the two teams have (almost!) never gotten along. They are the Hatfields and the McCoys of Major League Baseball.

The humid air of competitiveness is thick between the two factions. And neither side forgets easily. When longtime Cubs all-star Ron Santo signed with the Sox in 1972, he was greeted from the stands on Opening Day at Comiskey with this poster: "Welcome to the Major Leagues, Ron Santo."

White Sox fans tend to think Cubs fans are whiny yuppies who, like Red Sox fans until recently, moan about being "cursed" instead of taking their mediocrity in stride. These days, White Sox fans walk around with anti-Cubs T-shirts, including one that reads: "Cubs: Chokers since 1908."

For their part, Cubs fans tend to view White Sox rooters as fair-weather rednecks who only support their team when it is successful, and sometimes not even then. U.S. Cellular Field, the former New Comiskey Park, home of the White Sox, has not seen a lot of sellouts in recent days, even though the Sox had the best record in baseball from nearly day one of their 2005 season.

For the Cubs, the quest for respectability over the past several decades has had more ups and downs. Though they won their last World Championship in 1908, they have at least been *in* a few World Series since. They played and lost in the 1910, 1918, 1929, 1932, 1935, 1938, and 1945 Fall Classics. Add to that a spectacular collapse in 1969 and a heartbreaking defeat in the 2003 National League Championship Series. In other words, at least there's been something to grab on to, as disappointing as it has all turned out.

Plus, the Cubbies had their own theatrical production as an outlet for their angst. *Bleacher Bums*, which debuted in 1977, follows the fans of Wrigley's right-field bleachers as they hold on to the belief that "this is the year!" One wonders if the production would have done so well had the Cubs actually reached that holy grail.

Until 2005, the White Sox had been in just one World Series since 1919. That was that heady year in 1959, when the "Go-Go Sox" finally slid past the Yankees and the Cleveland Indians to claim the American League crown. But after a big start, fans were disappointed again when the Sox were downed by the Los Angeles Dodgers.

There were, to be sure, other playoff teams, in 1983, 1993, and 2000. But there were no Bill Buckner–esque moments in any of those series, no nail-biting, edge-of-your-seat games. The Sox just got beat.

That all ended, of course, not in Chicago, but in Houston, when the Sox brought home their first World Series title since 1917. That wasn't enough to give them the keys to the city, or at least to the hearts of *all* Chicago fans, but it gave them bragging rights that they can carry for a while.

Whose Town? Does Chicago Swing for the Cubs?

Overall, Chicago is clearly a Cubs town. The day before the 2005 World Series started, Bob Ryan, a columnist for the *Boston Globe*, noted that the playoffs hadn't generated the near-hysteria in Chicago that it had in Boston in 2004. In game two of this year's American League Championship Series, a disputed call in the ninth inning led to a Chicago victory, but there was no dancing in the streets afterward, no barroom crowds debating the finer points of the call into the wee hours of the morning. Umpire Doug Eddings ruled that Los Angeles Angel catcher Josh Paul didn't catch the ball when a third strike was called on Sox catcher A. J. Pierzynski, a call that eventually led to the winning run in a 2-1 game. The decision, which would have been rehashed for days afterward in Boston, noted Ryan, generated relatively little discussion. In fact, the biggest story of the 2005 World Series between the Sox and the Houston Astros was Astro second baseman Craig Biggio's wife getting attacked by a drunken White Sox fan.

White Sox fans believe the *Chicago Tribune*, whose parent company owns the Cubs, has something to do with the bias in popularity. When

Fans in the bleachers celebrate as Cub Jason Dubois blasts a three-run homer in the sixth inning to defeat the crosstown rival White Sox, 4–3 on May 22, 2005 at Wrigley.

asked by the Associated Press why the Sox didn't draw well despite a winning team, center fielder Aaron Rowand said simply, "WGN," which is the television station owned by the Tribune Company. The Cubs are on television much more often than the White Sox, his comment implied, and fans have responded accordingly.

In response, Cubs officials and fans note that the real secret is that the Cubs have done a better job marketing a lousy team over the years. While former Sox owner Bill Veeck was outfitting his teams in shorts and burning disco records in the 1970s, the Cubs ownership, including both the Wrigley family and the Tribune, worked hard to improve the concessions, parking, and seating at Wrigley Field.

Demographics also clearly play a part in why the Cubs draw better than the White Sox. Comiskey Park was constructed in 1910 in what at the time was one of the most affluent neighborhoods in Chicago, the Near South Side. In fact, many buildings constructed around that time are still standing, although most are in need of repair.

But as the twentieth century progressed, that neighborhood aged badly. The upkeep of these older buildings began to wane, and the neighborhood deteriorated. In addition, the Chicago stockyard railroad system is located on the eastern side of the Comiskey Park, and sixteen lanes of interstate highway lie not far from the western side. Not the greatest spot for a relaxing Sunday at the ballpark.

As the years passed, although the ballpark itself still generated some income, fewer and fewer businesses were established in that part of the city, particularly after World War II. Although crime rates in that part of Chicago were not greater overall than many areas, the perception was that the territory around Comiskey Park was not safe, a feeling that continues today. Some assume the Near South is not "family friendly" and that White Sox fans are thugs. Truth is, the crime rate has not risen appreciably, and in some areas near the ballpark it has dropped. Still, perception is reality to many fans.

Several high-profile events haven't helped the neighborhood's bad rap. In 2002, Kansas City coach Tom Gamboa was beaten by a father-and-son team at U.S. Cellular Field. And in 2003, an unruly fan tried to tackle an ump but was beaten back by several Sox players.

Perception aside, what *is* true is that businesses in that part of town have a smaller economic base with which to work and have difficulty succeeding. White Sox fans don't have a host of restaurants and post-game watering holes from which to choose. In that sense, the Near South isn't fan friendly.

Meanwhile, in the Wrigleyville (or Lakeville) section of town, the area in which Wrigley Field is located, the neighborhood feel has been retained for several generations. According to the U.S. Census survey in the 1980s and 1990s, real estate values were relatively modest, and younger families relocated to the area. These families continued to support the small businesses in that area. Today, the area around Wrigley Field thrives, and fans eagerly swarm to the ivy-covered stadium whether their team wins or loses.

It's All About the Team

Fans of both franchises are intensely loyal to their teams, and affiliations are passed down through the generations. Rare is the son who becomes a Cubs fan if his father and his father's father (or mother!) rooted for the Sox.

An abiding respect for the players is another aspect of Chicago fandom. In his autobiography, *Crash*, former Sox first baseman Dick Allen recalled that on the first day of spring training in 1972, his first year with the Sox (he'd previously played for the Phillies, Cardinals, and Dodgers), he was asked what people in Chicago should call him. Rich, Richie, or Dick? Allen admitted he was stunned. No one had ever asked him such a question. It was always "Richie," a name he loathed. So, given the chance, Allen asked the fans to call him "Dick." From that day on, cabbies, policemen, bartenders, and everyone in Chicago would say hi to Dick Allen. He resolved to repay the fans with his best effort, which he did. Allen was named MVP in 1972.

"They are great fans in Chicago," noted former pitcher Darold Knowles in Peter Golenbock's superb book *Wrigleyville*. Knowles threw for the Cubs from 1975 to 1976 but was presumably speaking about White Sox fans as well, since he also played in the American League for several years. "They will boo you when you do bad, but they are not like Philly fans. Philly fans have the reputation of waiting for you to do something wrong so they can jump on you. In Chicago, they want you to win. They root for you, and if you're bad, they'll boo you, but they will turn right around and cheer you. Chicago fans will cheer the opposing team if they do something good, and that's great. They are baseball people."

Perhaps the most famous Cubs fan is *Washington Post* columnist George Will. Will is an unabashed baseball fanatic and has written a few books on the subject, including *Men at Work: The Craft of Baseball* and *Bunts*.

The White Sox' most famous fan was probably Ted "Double-Duty" Radcliffe. A well-known player in his own right, Radcliffe was a star of the Negro Leagues in the 1930s. He loved the game and loved Comiskey Park, and had even played there as a member of the Chicago American Giants. Radcliffe was a frequent visitor to the park and the White Sox dugout right up until his death in 2005 at the age of 103.

The Cubs have the dubious honor of having one of the most infamous fans in Chicago baseball history, perhaps in all of Chicago sports history. The honor (or dishonor, as it may be) belongs to Steve Bartman, a relatively inoffensive, twenty-six-year-old Cubs fan who decided, in 2003, to try to catch a foul ball during game six of the National League Championship Series, and in the process inadvertently deflected it from left fielder Moises Alou. The Cubs, who had been leading the series three games to two, lost that game. They went on to lose game seven, which shut them out of the World Series for the fifty-eighth consecutive year.

And then there are the celebrities whose allegiances are tracked in the glare of a bright spotlight. While an ordinary fan might be able to switch his allegiance from one team to another relatively anonymously, celebrities like actor John Cusack are subject to closer scrutiny. Cusack is a Chicago native and longtime city baseball fan, but he played a member of the White Sox (well, the Black Sox, actually) in the movie *Eight Men Out*. You'd think the White Sox would treat him well for his efforts and court his allegiance to their side of the city. Nope. Cusack was famously turned down when he asked for tickets to a White Sox playoff game in 2005. Team owner Jerry Reinsdorf, still peeved that Cusack had publicly supported the Cubs in their near-successful 2003 season, said that Cusack "used to be a White Sox fan."

Those are harsh words. But, as we said, there are no diplomats in foxholes.

White Sox fans made the worthwhile trip to Houston and rejoiced as their team won the Fall Classic on October 26, 2005.

A Divided City

The 2005 postseason was witness to an interesting phenomenon: Cubs fans rooting for the White Sox. National columnist Mike Baumann first noted it in a column on MLB.com on October 18, just after the White Sox had eliminated the Los Angeles Angels in the American League Championship Series.

Baumann explained that he had made a crack about Cubs fans never rooting for the South Side team in the American League. He then received a torrent of e-mails refuting his point.

"Cubs fans," wrote Baumann, "insisted they would be rooting for the White Sox to win the World Series. Not because they were fair-weather fans and not because they were tired of disappointment. No, Cubs fans (some of them anyway) will be rooting for the White Sox in the World Series because it will be good for the city of Chicago and for Chicago baseball."

As if to support Baumann's description of a mostly unified town, avowed Cubs fan Michael Wilbon, one half of ESPN's *Pardon the Interruption* team, was spotted wearing a White Sox shirt just before the start of the World Series.

Not all Cubs fans are running to the souvenir racks for their Sox shirts, however. Many are disappointed at the success of their century-old, crosstown rivals. And when it looked for a moment that a White Sox–Cardinals World Series was imminent in 2005, Chicago columnist Mike Downey polled some Chi-town celebs on who they'd root for. (Note that the Cardinals are the Cubs' biggest rivals.) Asking a Cubs fan to choose between the Sox and the Cards is like asking whether you'd like brussels sprouts or boiled cauliflower for dessert.

Comedian Tom Dreesen came up with this answer: "There's no doubt in my mind that Cubs fans would root for St. Louis. In my opinion, there is no greater rivalry in the world than White Sox versus Cubs. The last thing a Cub fan wants is for the Sox to become World Series champs before the Cubs do. It would break their hearts. Believe me, they'd be for the Cardinals."

Now Chi-Sox vs. Astros . . . that's a whole different story. ★

*White Sox catcher Jamie Burke covers home plate
against the sliding Corey Patterson of the Cubs.
The Cubs won the interleague game held on July 2,
2004, at Wrigley, defeating the White Sox 6–2.*

Conclusion ★ ★ ★

Chicago has been a baseball town for more than a century, and a big-league baseball town at that. Which made it all the more rewarding when at last—at sweet, sweet last—the White Sox scored what had so long eluded the city: a World Series Championship. October 26, 2005, marked the end of decades-long drought for the team and its beleaguered fans, as the Sox trounced the Houston Astros with a resounding four-game sweep.

Meanwhile, as the twenty-first century enters the sprawling stretch of a new millennium and the Cubs' 2003 playoff memories fade into history, Cubs fans continue to hold their collective breath, pinning their hopes on solid pitching staffs, top-notch fielders, and remarkable hitters. That is, the very same elements baseball fans have been pinning their hopes on since the game's inception. And though it's been almost a hundred years since the Cubbies last hoisted a World Series banner, you won't find this town giving up its North Side dream. Their Sox showed the world it could be done; why couldn't it be done again? Besides, for baseball fans, hope remains one of those things that only grows stronger with time.

A final anecdote attesting to the loyalty of Chicago's baseball lovers: In September of 1971, White Sox third baseman Bill Melton socked his thirty-third home run to win the American League home run title. It was a fairly important event, as it was the first time a White Sox player had ever claimed the crown.

After the game, a White Sox fan came into the clubhouse and presented Melton with the ball—a seemingly remarkable act, when such balls could have been auctioned off for a decent sum, even in those days.

But as it turned out, the lucky catch was less remarkable than it might have been in a town less obsessed, among crowds less dedicated. As this White Sox fan excitedly told Melton, snagging balls in the stands was nothing new—he reported that it was his 490th ball to date.

And likely not his last. ★

Index ★ ★ ★

Abbot, Spencer, 144
Adams, Franklin Pierce, 23–24
African American players *see also* Negro Leagues
    hotel restrictions on, 33, 90
    signing of, 33
All-American Girls Professional Baseball League
    (AAGPBL), 94–98, *95, 96, 97, 99*
Allen, Dick, 65, 133, 164
All-Star Games
    Major League, 58, 90, 108, *109*
    Negro League, 90–93, 108, 110
Allyn, Arthur, Jr., 63
Allyn, John, 64
Alou, Moises, 42, *42*, 116, 165
Altrock, Nick, 21
American League, 44, 47, 61, 83, 110
Anson, Cap, *15*, 17–18, *19*, 20, 122
Aparicio, Luis, 134, *136*
Appling, Luke, 58, 134, *135*
Arabian Gulf Little League, 79
attendance, game *see also* fans
    Negro League All-Star games, 90
    New Comiskey Park, 111
    records, 61, 66
    women's baseball, 96, 97

Badger, Walter, *17*
Baines, Harold, 76, 138, *165*
Baker, Eugene, 33
Banks, Ernie, *33*, 33–34, 115, 125
Barnes, Roscoe C., 16, 17, *17, 18*
Barnett, Charlene, 97, *99*
Bartell, Dick, 146
Bartman, Steve, *42*, 42–43, 105, 116, 165
"Baseball's Sad Lexicon," 24
Baumann, Mike, 167
Beckert, Glenn, 35, 124
Berger, Wally, 146
Billy Goat Tavern, 32
Black Sox scandal, 53–57, 116, *117*
Bleacher Bums (play), 160
Bluege, Oswald Lewis, 146
Blues Brothers, The (movie), 102
Blum, Geoff, 72
Borowy, Hank, 32, 116
Boston Red Sox, 25, 43
Boston Red Stockings, 17, 19
Brickhouse, Jack, 156, *159*

broadcasters, 156–159
Brooklyn Dodgers, 33
Brown, Mordecai Centennial, *22, 23*, 48, 112, 129
Buehrle, Mark, 69
Burke, Jaime, *169*
Burkina Faso Little League, 80
Burns, Tommy, 20, 21

"called shot" home run, 29, 31, 105, 116, *118*
Caray, Harry, 156, *157*, 158, 160
Carrasquel, Alfonso, 134
Cavarretta, Phil, 32, 36, 122
Chance, Frank, 20, 23, 24, *24*, 48, 122
Chicago, city of, 10, 43, 76, 162 *see also* fans
Chicago American Giants, *86*, 87–89, *88*
Chicago Colleens, 97–98
Chicago Columbia Giants, 84, 87
Chicago Cubs
    Bartman game, *42*, 42–43, 105, 116, 165
    controversial games, 21, 23
    fans, 43, 160, 162, 164, 167
    goat curse, 32, 36
    management, 26, 29, 35, 37
    1906 World Series, 21, 48–49, 112
    1908 World Series, 23, 112
    ownership change, 24, 25, 29, 37
    rivals, 40, 167
    as underachievers, 14, 43, 160
    Weeghman Field, 24, 25, 82
    Wrigley Field, 102, *104*, 104–106, *106*, 164
Chicago Defender, 90
Chicago Tribune, 162–163
Chicago Tribune Corporation, 37, 163
Chicago Unions, 84
Chicago Whales, 81–82
Chicago White Sox
    Black Sox scandal, 53–57, *56*, 116, *117*
    fans, 160, 163–165, *166*
    financial difficulties, 58–59
    Hitless Wonders, 20–21, 44, 112
    home parks, 67–70, 107–108, 110, *110*, 111
    management, 47, 48, 57, 59, 64, 65, 66–67, 69
    1906 World Series, 21, 48–49, 112
    1917 World Series, 1917, 50–52, 115
    origins, 46
    ownership changes, 58, 61, 63, 64, 65, 66
    salaries, 52
    season lineups, 50, 56, 57, 59, 61–63, 69, 70

team names, 44, 47, 59
team photographs, *45, 54*
2005 World Series, 44, 70–75, 112, *114*, 115
uniforms, 65
Chicago White Sox Park, 87, 108
Chicago White Stockings, *15*, 16–20
Chi-Feds, 81
Cicotte, Eddie, 50, 53, 55, 56, 140
Cincinnati Reds, 53–55, 75
Clancy, Jim, 146–147
Clarkson, John, *15*, 18, 131
coaches, 34–35, 96
Cobb, Ty, 21, 119, 137
College of Coaches, 34–35
Collins, Eddie, 50, 52, *132*, 133
Combs, Earle, *30*
Comiskey, Charlie *45*, 46, 49, 52–53, 57–58,
    90, *113*
Comiskey, Chuck, 61, 63
Comiskey, Grace, 59, 61
Comiskey, J. Louis, 58
Comiskey Park
    All-Star Game, 90, 108, *109*
    circus, *60*
    construction costs, 110
    Disco Demolition Night, 65–66, 119
    historical moments, 108, 110
    history, 49–50, 107–108
    neighborhood, 163
    night games, 108
    scoreboards, 63, 108, *110*, 159
commissioners, baseball, 83
Crash (Allen), 164
Crede, Joe, *3, 73*
Cuban X Giants, 87
curses, 32, 36
Cusack, John, 165

Dahl, Steve, 66
Dahlen, Bill, 20
Dalrymple, Abner, 18
Damn Yankees (play), 64
Dapkus, Eleanor, 96, 98
Dasso, Frank, 144
Davis, Zachary Taylor, 82, 107
Dawson, Andre, 34, 125
death threats, 23, 56
Dellinger, Harold, 83

Detroit Tigers, 21, 31, 32, *32*
DiMaggio, Joe, 31
Disco Demolition Night, *65,* 65–66, 119
Doby, Larry, 110
Donovan, Dick, 63
Dotson, Rich, 66
double no-hit games, 104
Doyle, Dorothy, 97
Dreesen, Tom, 167
Drysdale, Don, 63
Durocher, Leo, 35–36
Dye, Jermaine, 112

Earnshaw, George, 26
Ed Sullivan Show, The, 153
Eight Men Out (movie), 165
Einhorn, Eddie, 66, 110
Elgin Classic Little League, 79
Elson, Bob, 156, *158*
Evers, Johnny, 20, 21, 24, *24,* 48, 124
exhibition games, 18–19, 96, 98
exploding scoreboard, 63, 108, 159

Faber, Urban Clarence, 140
Falkenberg, Frederick, 148
fans *see also* attendance, game
    devotion, 10, 43, 164–165
    game interference, 42
    loyalty, 164
    photographs, *9, 65, 161, 162, 166*
    rivalry, 160
    team popularity, 162–163
    2005 World Series, 167
Federal League, 24, 81–83, *82*
Feller, Bob, 110
Fenway Park, 25, 102
Findlay Sluggers, 84
fireworks, 108
Fisk, Carlton, 66, *67,* 115, 137
fixed games, 53–57, *56,* 116, *117*
Florida Marlins, 42, 116
Florreich, Lois, 97
Ford C. Frick broadcasting award, 156
Foster, Andrew, 87–90, *88*
Foster, Bill, *91*
foul balls, *42,* 42–43, 104, 105, 116, 165
Fox, Nellie, 59, 133
Fraser, Charles, 148

free agency, 37
Freeman, Barry, 78
FUNdamentals arcade, 111

gambling, 53–57, 116, *117*
Gandil, Chick, 50, 53
Garcia, Freddy, 72
Garland, Jon, 69
gasoline restrictions, wartime, 32
Gehrig, Lou, 29, *30*
Gianfrancisco, Philomena, 98
Gibson, Josh, *92*
Gilmore, James, 81
Gleason, Kid, 53, 55
Golenbock, Peter, 164
Gore, George, 18, 19
Goshorn, Kevin, 79
Gottselig, Johnny, 96
Grace, Mark, 122, *123*
Grant, Charlie, 84, *85*
Great Chicago Fire, 16, 116
Green, Dallas, 37–38
Greenberg, Hank, 32
Greenlee, Gus, 90
Griffith, Clark, 20, 47, 48
Grim, Charlie, 29, 116, 126
Groth, Johnny, 148
Guillen, Ozzie, 14, 69, 134
Gullickson, Bill, 76
Gutierrez, Ricky, 115

Hack, Stan, 124–125
Harnett, Ann, 96
Harris, Willie, 112, *165*
Hart, James A., 20
Hartnett, Charles Leo, *30,* 105, 112, 115, *118,*
    128, 129
Hawkins, Andy, 110
Henderson, Rickey, 148
Hendrix, Claude, 25, 81
Herman, Billy, 124, *124*
Hernandez, Orlando, 70
Herzog, Buck, 52
Hitless Wonders, 20–21, 44, 112
Homer in the Gloamin', 105, 112, 115
home runs
    "called shot," 29, 31, 105, 116, *118*
    by catchers, 105, 112, 115

in franchise history, 133
    title holders, 115, 125, 126, 168
Hornsby, Rogers, 26, 28, *28,* 29
Hoyt, LaMarr, 66
Hulbert, William A., 16
Hundley, Randy, 35

Iguchi, Tadahito, 70
Illinois State Little League championships, *79,* 80
Isbell, Frank, 21, 48, 49
ivy, Wrigley Field, 104

Jackie Robinson West Little League, 78–79
Jackson, Joe, 50, 52, 53–57, 116, 138
Jenkins, Ferguson, 35, 131
Jenkins, Horace, 89
Jenks, Bobby, 72, 75
Johnson, Ban, 10, 46, *46*
Johnson, Grant, 84, 87
Jones, Fielder, *47,* 48

Kankakee Jacyees Little League, 80
Kansas City Monarchs, 93
Kappel, John, 78
Kelly, Michael Joseph, *15,* 18–19, 129, *129*
Kerr, Dickie, *53,* 55
Kessinger, Don, 125
Kittle, Ron, 66
Kling, Johnny, 21
Kluszewski, Ted, *62,* 63
Knowles, Darold, 164
knuckleball pitchers, 141
Konerko, Paul, 69, 72, 75
Kotowicz, Irene, 98

Ladies Night, 26
Landis, Kenesaw Mountain, 56, 83, 116
Lane, Frank, 59
LaRussa, Tony, 66–67
lawsuits, 83
Leibrandt, Charlie, 149
LeJeune, Sheldon, 142, *142*
Leland, Frank, 84, 87
Leland Giants, 87
Lelivelt, Jack, 142
Lenard, Jo, 98
Leverenz, Walter, 144, *145*
Lidge, Brad, 72

lights, stadium, 105–106, 108
Lindstrom, Freddie, 149–150
Little League, 76–80
Lockman, Whitey, 36
Lollar, Sherm, 59
Long, Herman, 150
Lopez, Al, 59–61, 64
Los Angeles Angels of Anaheim, 70–72
Los Angeles Dodgers, 61
Luzinski, Greg, 66, 150
Lycoming Dairy Little League, 76
Lynn, Fred, 110, 150, *151,* 153
Lyons, Jimmie, 93
Lyons, Ted, 57, 140, *140*

Macias, Angel, 78
Maddux, Greg, 131
Madlock, Bill, 36
Maris, Roger, 115
Mathewson, Christy, 21
Maynard Midgets Little League, 76
Mays, Carl, 25
McCarthy, Joe, 26, 28, 119
McCormick, Harry, 21
McDowell, Jack, 67, *68,* 140
McGraw, Charles, 79
McGraw, John, 51, 84
McGwire, Mark, 28, 40, 115
McLain, Denny, 153
McManus, Marty, 153
McVey, Cal, 16
media
    broadcasters, 156–159
    popularity biases, 162–163
    radio broadcast rights, 25
    radio promotions, *65,* 65–66, 119
Melton, Bill, 65, 137
Men at Work: The Craft of Baseball
    (Will), 165
Merkle, Fred, 21, 23, 25
Metzler, Alex, *10*
Meyerhoff, Arthur, 96
Midwestern Colored Championship, 84
Minoso, Minnie, *58,* 59, 139
Mitchell, Bobby, 76
modern ballparks, 111
Monroe, Bill, 89

National Association, 16
National League, 16–17, 83
National League Championship Series, 38
Neale, Earle, 53
Negro Leagues *see also* African American players
    All-Star Games, 90–93, 108, 110
    disbanding of, 93
    history, 84
    teams, 84, *85, 86,* 87–89
Negro National League, 89
New Comiskey Park, 67–70, 108, 110, *110*
New York Giants, 21, 23, 112
New York Mets, 35–36
New York Yankees, 29, 57, 64, 75
night games, 105–106, 108

O'Day, Hank, 21, 23
O'Dowd, Annie, 98
off-season series games, 18–19, 96, 98
Ordonez, Magglio, 69, 139, *139*

Pafko, Andy, 126
Paige, Satchel, 93
Patterson, Corey, *169*
Patterson, Pat, 93
Paul, Josh, 70
Perlick, Edythe, 96, *96,* 98
Peters, Gary, 64
Peterson, Fred, 153
Petway, Bruce, 89
Pfister, Jack, 23
Philadelphia Athletics, 16, 26
Piazza, Mike, 115
Pierce, Billy, 59, 63, 141
Piersall, Jimmy, 159
Pierzynski, A. J., 70
Pipp, Wally, *152,* 153–154
Pirok, Pauline, 98
pitchers' duels, 72
Pittsburgh Courier, 90
Pittsburgh Pirates, 21
Pittsburgh Rebels, 82
Pizarro, Juan, 64
Podsednik, Scott, 72, *74,* 115
popularity biases, 162–163
Powell, Pat, 93
Powers, John T., 81
Powers, Mike, 78

press *see* media
Prior, Mark, 42
promotions
    circus, *60*
    Disco Demolition Night, *65,* 65–66, 119
    Ladies Night, 26
Pruess, Earl, 146
Puckett, Kirby, 154, *154*

Quarrels, Norrice, 79

Radar, Doug, 154
Radcliffe, Ted, *92,* 93, 165, *165*
radio, 25, *65,* 65–66, 119, 156–159
Reagan, Ronald, 159
Redding, Dick, 89
Reilley, Alexander, 142, *144*
Reinsdorf, Jerry, 66, 110, 165
Robinson, Jackie, Jr., *80*
Robinson, Jackie, Sr., 33, *80,* 93
Robles, Alex, 80
Rockford Peaches, 97
Root, Charlie, 26, 105, 116
Rowand, Aaron, 69
Ruth, Babe
    All-Star Game home run, 58
    with Boston Red Sox, 25
    "called shot," 29, 31, 105, 116, *118*
    with New York Yankees, 29, *30*
Ryan, Bob, 162

salaries, 52, 87
Sandberg, Ryne, *37,* 38, 124
Santo, Ron, 34, *34,* 125, 159
Saperstein, Abe, 108
Saturday Evening Post, 76
Schalk, Ray, 55, 57, 137, *138*
Schillace, Clara, 96, 98
Schoendist, Red, 110
Schorling, John, 89
Schorling's Park, *89,* 89–90
scoreboards, 63, 104, 108, 159
Scout Seating areas, 111
Sells, Ken, 94
Sewell, Joe, 29, *30*
Shaw, Bobby, 63
Sheehan, Jack, 94
Shivley, Twila, 98

Sianis, William, 32
Simmons, Al, 108
Skowron, Bill, 154
Smith, Lee, *130,* 131
Smith, Lonnie, 154
Sosa, Sammy, 38–40, *39,* 126
South Side Park, *48,* 107
Spalding, Albert, 16–17, *17,* 20, 24
Spalding, J. Walter, 17
Spalding's Sporting Store, 17
Speed-O-Meter, 111
spring training, 97
Stanky, Eddie, 64
Staub, Rusty, *34*
stealing players, 81, 83
Steinfeldt, Harry, 48
St. Louis Brown Stockings, 18
St. Louis Cardinals, 37, 40, 167
St. Louis Saints, 46
St. Louis Terriers, 82
Stock, Milt, 155
Stotz, Carl, 76
Stratton, Monty, 58
Street, Bryan, 78
Sutcliffe, Rick, 36, 119
Sutter, Bruce, 36–37

Taft, Charles, 24
"Take Me Out to the Ball Game," *157,* 158
Taylor Northwest Little League, 78
theatrical productions, 64, 160
Thigpen, Bobby, 67
Thomas, Frank, 67, *71,* 133
Thompson, Jim, 67
Tinker, Joe, 20, 24, *24,* 48, 81
"Tinker to Evers to Chance" (Adams), 24, *24*
Toney, Fred, 105
Torriente, Christobal, 89
Total Baseball (Dellinger), 83
turf, artificial, 108

Uribe, Juan, 75
U.S. Cellular Field, 69–70, 111

Vaughn, James, 25, 104
Veeck, Mary Frances, 65
Veeck, Mike, *65,* 65–66, 119
Veeck, William, Sr., 25–26, 61, 104

Veeck, William Lewis, Jr., 61, 63, 65

Waddell, Rube, 87
Wagner, Honus, 21
Walsh, Ed, 21, 49–50, *50,* 107, 141
Warneke, Lon, 29, 131
Wasiak, Stanley, 144
Weaver, George, 137
Weeghman, Charles, 24, 25, 82, 83, 102
Weeghman Park, 24, 25, 82
Weintraub, Philip, 144
Western League, 46, 47
Westlawn Little League, 78, 79–80
White, Guy Harris, 141
White, Jim, 16
White Sox Park, 87
Wickware, Frank, 89
Wilhelm, Hoyt, 141
Will, George, 165
Williams, Billy, 34
Williams, Claude, 50, 53, 55–56
Williams, Kenny, 69
Williamson, Edward, 18
Wilson, Lewis Robert, 26, 28, *28,* 126, *127*
Wood, Jimmy, 16
Wood, Kerry, *41,* 42, 115
Wood, Wilbur, 141
World Series
     1906 (Cubs vs. White Sox), 21, 48–49, 112
     1907 (Cubs vs. Tigers), 21, *21*
     1908 (Cubs vs. Tigers), 23, 112
     1910 (Cubs vs. Athletics), 23
     1917 (White Sox vs. Giants), 50–52, 115
     1919 (White Sox vs. Reds), 52–57, *56,* 116, *117*
     1929 (Cubs vs. Athletics), 26, *27*
     1932 (Cubs vs. Yankees), 29
     1935 (Cubs vs. Tigers), 31
     1945 (Cubs vs. Tigers), 32
     1959 (White Sox vs. Dodgers), 61–62
     2005 (White Sox vs. Astros), 44, 70–75, 112, *114,* 115
World War I, 52
World War II, 32, 59, 94, 105
World's Colored Championship Series, 87
Wright, Harry, 17
Wrigley, Philip K., 29, *29,* 31, 34, 37, 94, 104
Wrigley, William, 25, *27,* 29, 37
Wrigley, William, Jr., 104
Wrigley Field, 102, *104,* 104–106, *106,* 164

Wrigleyville, 102, 164
Wrigleyville (Golenbock), 164
Wyatt, Ralph, 93
Wynn, Early, 61, 63

Yearick, Allen, 76

Zwilling, Dutch, 81

Photo Credits ★★★

Acknowledgments ★ ★ ★

Like a baseball team, a book like this is a team effort. First and foremost, my thanks to my editor at becker&meyer!, Avra Romanowitz, who managed this bicoastal effort with grace, extreme patience and good humor. Those qualities are the best for which any writer can ask. My thanks also to Conor Risch, another editor at becker&meyer!, who got this whole ball rolling in the first place. Also, thanks to Shayna Ian, a very gifted photo researcher, who made this book look terrific.

Out East, my thanks to the folks at the Baseball Hall of Fame, who earn more of my respect for their professionalism and stupendous volume of information every time I need information. Thanks also to the keepers of the archives at the Boston Public Library and the New York Public Library. I always leave both places wishing I had more time to just absorb the information on their microfilm. Like maybe a year or so. Also, a tip of the hat to the Society for American Baseball Research, whose many publications are simply indispensable for a researcher.

On a personal note, as always, my deepest appreciation goes out to my parents and four sisters and their respective spouses for their support. It's hard to imagine doing these books without them. ★

About the Author ★★★

Derek Gentile is the unofficial baseball historian of Berkshire County, as well as the author of a number of baseball books, including *The Complete Chicago Cubs*, *The Complete Boston Red Sox* and *The Complete New York Yankees*. He lives in Great Barrington, Massachusetts. ★